A PENNY
AND AN EGG

The early years of a country boy

W J H Olding

Edited by Gill Breeze

DEDICATION

W J H Olding
1925 – 2005

In 1998 Jack Olding, my dad, printed his memories of growing up in the small Cornish village of Blunts, and gave copies to his family. It has been treasured by us all since then. Now it's time to create a more durable copy of this treasure.

Working on his memoirs for publishing as a book has been a labour of love. I hope you will enjoy reading it as much as we have.

Edited for publication by Gill Breeze (2014)

CONTENTS

CHAPTER 1 – THE VILLAGE

Most places changed in some way during the last century. Probably more changes have taken place during the period since the outbreak of war in 1939 than at any stage of history. Nowhere have these changes become more evident than in the rural areas. Many country villages, who, not so long ago, had a leisurely way of life, have become almost completely deserted where local schools have closed, village shops have disappeared and the younger generation moved to areas of full employment. Many villages have become mini satellite towns for the rich who have built mock Georgian houses or developed estates of over decorated bungalows. A few villages have survived by allowing limited development of vacated cottages. Cottages that were once homes to farm workers and their families, with no modern amenities, now offer weekend peace and relaxation to city dwellers, who have installed all the modern equipment that is now available to make life a little more comfortable.

The local community has not lost out completely. They have been able to share the improved amenities. Despite their views of "weekenders", there must be very few who would return to the old way of life with no mains water, and paraffin lamps for lighting. Life without the television in a rural area is almost unthinkable. Without the influx of outside wealth, it is likely that the majority of the old houses would have collapsed long ago through neglect and would have been lost forever.

The motorcar is available to everyone now, so the country dweller is within reach of the shops and entertainments of the city, making things a little more evenly balanced.

My introduction to the little village of Blunts was as a toddler under two years old, when my parents moved to the little smallholding of St. Mellion. That cottage is now destined to support the approach to the eighteenth hole of the St. Mellion Golf Club.

It must have been a relief for all concerned when we moved out from that little two up and two down cottage at Dunstan. My mother's mother and father lived there, when Grandfather, John Billing was horseman at

Dunstan Farm. With them at home was my mother, with brothers Jack, Eric, Fred and the youngest Cecil, along with the youngest daughter Winifred. The eldest sister Edith and the oldest son Arthur were away in Service. When Grandmother Georgina Billing died, my mother Louise kept house for all the family. After the war (1914-1918) mother and father were married and I was born to make life a little more crowded. Mother and father moved to Holwood farm cottages for a brief period (where Ray was born), until our cottage at Blunts was ready for occupation. Aunt Win took over looking after the Billing family at Dunstan with help from Aunt Ede (Edith) until Grandfather Billing got married again.

So what would I find at Blunts, the little village off the beaten track in East Cornwall that I left over half a century ago? Not easy to find, it is sited near the centre point of a triangle formed by the market towns of Saltash, Callington and Liskeard.

Although it was not large enough to be a real village it was always referred to as "the village" by everyone who lived there, and by all the surrounding farms and houses. It was built beside the road that runs from Saltash to St. Ive. It meets the road from Callington to Tideford to form a "T" junction at the top of the village.

To stand at the centre of that "T" junction, as I did earlier this year (1992) was like being taken back in time to the day that I left it all behind in 1936. The mere fact that I could stand in the middle of the "T" junction was something of an achievement. Very few cars pass this way even today. Whichever route you take to get to the village, narrow roads are the only way in or out. Roads that are only cart width with the occasional passing place dug out from the high hedges are a left over from Victorian days, when most of the village was built. Roads which in my young days we looked upon as being good and very modern are still there, and equivalent to a "C" or at best a "B" Class road, but mostly unclassified.

Although most of the village is classified as Victorian, there are older parts of the village still in use. The house (Forge Cottage) that in my day was occupied by Granny Jane, who we will meet later, is dated around 1620. The building that we occupied as a corn store, before which it had been in use as a stable, and which in the 18th Century was converted from a cottage to a blacksmith shop, is reputed to be 16th century.

The original blacksmiths shop on the St. Ive road is reputed to be even older. The very old cottage at the top of the village was an early 16th Century building.

Just one field away on the North side of the village was one of the two old Manor Houses of the parish, mentioned in the Doomsday Book.

Penpol at that time, held "land for 3 ploughs, 4 slaves, 6 villagers and 6 smallholders. There were three acres of meadow, six acres of woodland and thirty acres of pasture". We knew it as a well-run farm with a large farmhouse that had about thirty windows at the front. The other old manor house in the parish, Leigh, about two miles from the village, on the Tebrown lane, had "land for four ploughs, two slaves, ten smallholders, plus a meadow of two acres, one acre of woodland and five acres of pasture".

The actual village can boast no fine buildings or claim to fame. The parish of Quethiock in which the village lies does have a history, which started in the eighth or ninth Century. (A very fine Wheel Head Cross erected at that time, still stands near the village Church.) Considering this, there is every possibility that there were much older settlements in the vicinity.

The village in my days consisted of just eight houses, six of them built on the left side of the road if approached from Saltash in the South. On the right hand side at the top of the village there were two semi-detached houses that had been converted into one. A slate wall surrounded the house and large garden. The first building on the St. Ive (East) side of the "T" junction was a little corrugated iron Mission Church, erected at the turn of the century. Next was the village blacksmiths shop, with a huge steel disc laid on the ground outside the door, where wheels for carts and wagons from all the surrounding farms were fitted with iron tyres, after repair in the adjoining carpenter shop. Attached to the blacksmith's shop beside the road was the one and only garage for a private car in the village.

Situated in a huge garden beside the carpenter shop was an ex World War 1 Territorial Army hut, which had seen service as the Local Drill Hall, Stores and Recruiting station and in my young days, as a storage depot and distribution point for corn and fertiliser.

The only buildings on the right approaching the village from Saltash, were a shippon of 1920's construction, attached to the corn store cum stable, converted from an old blacksmith shop, which in turn had been converted from an old 16th Century cottage, mentioned earlier. This was the full extent of the village where I was to spend the first eleven years of my life.

Probably the most historic thing that ever happened to the village of Blunts in recent times was the auction of most of the village and the surround farms in 1919.

After the 1914/1918 War the Government introduced the Land Settlement (Facilities) Act of 1919. Under this Act the County Councils were encouraged to buy any farms or properties that were capable of sub division to form Small Holdings to be let to returning Servicemen. The whole cost of the Properties and a proportion of losses incurred for a period of six years, from March 31st 1920 would be borne by the Ministry of Agriculture.

At that time the whole area (with very few exceptions) was owned by the Squire, William Coryton of Pentille Castle near St. Mellion, and the whole was known as the Quethiock Estate.

On August 14th 1919 the whole Estate was offered for Sale by Public Auction at the Royal Hotel, Plymouth. Needless to say, very few local farmers or householders could outbid the Men From the Council, with their seemingly bottomless purse. The largest and best farms were bought by the Ministry, while others were bought up by wealthy landowners from outside the area. This was an auction that was not conducted in the way normally associated with the code of rural life in those days. If a sitting tenant was making a reasonable bid for property, none of his neighbours would outbid him and make him homeless. All that changed at this auction. The village of Blunts mostly consisted of cottages that were part of the farms that were up for Auction, whilst some cottages were let to Tenants of the Squire. One or two Tenants were successful in buying their own cottages but most passed to the County, as part of the larger farm. The days of a big Mortgage were not yet with us, at least not as we know it today. Deposits were usually a sum mutually agreed between Buyer and Seller, with a short repayment period, maybe only over five years. The usual mortgage was the agreement of landowners and others, who put up their property as security for a loan, usually from a Bank, often without a fixed period of repayment.

It was usual at that time for smallholdings to be of a convenient size for the man to follow his own occupation and his wife to run the day-to-day small tasks, such as poultry feeding, collecting eggs, and collecting and housing stock at the end of the day. Even the care of grazing cows by the roadside for a few hours a day fell to the smallholder's wife. The remainder of jobs were carried out at the end of the men's working day or before his work started in the mornings. With the feeding of stock, plus milking and mucking out of cowsheds and stables it meant long hours of hard work. All the smallholders were not farm workers but most were connected in some way to the farming community. There were sawyers, wheelwrights, carpenters, millers and masons, most of who saw some change in their life. In total, twenty-eight farms from the area were auctioned on that day, plus many cottages. The cottage we lived in was allocated two fields, one on the opposite side of the road, along with the corn store and shippon mentioned earlier, the other a few hundred yards on the road towards St. Ive. In all it formed a smallholding of about eight acres, about the average size intended by the Ministry.

Some of the other cottages forfeited their land for various reasons. For some would-be tenants the land was situated too far away from the dwelling, others had no buildings to house stock, or the tenant had some disability that prevented him from farming, even on a small scale. Any surplus fields were eagerly bought and often returned to the farm from which it had originally been taken, or added to another tenant's allocation of land.

To assist in making smallholdings of the required acreage, it was necessary in some cases, to divide large fields into convenient sizes, by the erection of fences. The large field at the top of the village was one of those divided. The largest portion of the field, bordering Broad Road, was known as our "Top Field", where we drove our cows to and fro every day to graze.

Broad Road, despite its name was not very wide, but had a very wide grass verge where householders were free to graze their cattle. It was many years later that the road was widened to become a "B" class road. Other alterations carried out by the new County owners included the building of farm buildings and fencing off a farmyard with stout timbers and the building of some shippons to form a dairy farm at the top of what we called Roosts Hill. All County owned cottages were classified as "Holdings" even if no land was rented with the cottage. Probably just one way of typing up loose ends as far as the County Council were concerned.

CHAPTER 2 – THE VILLAGERS

Perhaps it would be convenient at this point to mention a few of the people who lived in the village and how they earned a living. Mr. and Mrs. Wythe lived in the first house on the left as you entered the village from the Saltash direction. Mrs. Wythe was the official caretaker of the Chapel, but Mr. Wythe spent a lot of time helping her. They were not originally from Cornwall but had come from the London area during the War. Mr. Wythe had been wounded during the War and wore a leather support on his left arm and hand. He was the local postman, and every morning went off to Tideford on his red Post Office bike to collect the mail for the district. His return route would take him to all the little hamlets and farms. Tideford Cross, Cutmere, Cutcrew, Trenance and many isolated houses, to deliver the mail he had collected at Tideford.

It was the recognised thing that during his visits to these isolated places he would collect mail from where there no collection points and pop them into the Post Box at Blunts to be collected by the evening mail van. He was a nice slim gentleman and had a very small face. It was not very often that you saw him without his pipe, always held in his mouth so that it pointed forwards and downwards. There was usually a dewdrop on the end of his nose that caused a little hilarity amongst the school children that he met. He was a very genial sort of man, and took jokes about his dewdrop with a smile.

Mrs. Wythe was a short rotund lady, going a bit grey, who was always ready to stop and talk. A very homely lady, always ready to lend a helping hand. They had two sons, one a little older than myself, Victor, and an older son whose name I cannot recall. They were the proud owners of one of the two wireless sets (not radios in those days) in the village and would, on special occasions, invite my mother, father, myself and brother Ray in to listen to it. It was usually a very crackly reception and I cannot recall ever hearing any programme that I could understand. Mr. Wythe always listened in on a pair of earphones, but everyone else had to listen via the loudspeakers. He spent an awful lot of time putting up higher and longer aerials in an effort to improve reception, but it was all a bit futile when you considered the age of the receiver. I seem to remember Mr. Wythe buying the set second hand and bringing it home on the front of his Post Office bicycle. It was a bit primitive, even for those days. Just like a black box with knobs along the front, and a separate horn shaped speaker on a long wire. As a bit of a wireless enthusiast, Mr. Wythe had a couple of Crystal sets that he occasionally brought out to demonstrate to boys.

The largest house in the village was occupied, in my very early days by the Flashman family, who ran the small dairy farm that had been created at the tope of Roosts Hill, on the Tideford Road. The family were all grown up and moved away when I was about four years old. I can remember that there were two girls, Maisey and Edna and three boys, Jim, Edwin and Boysey. I did meet up with one, Jim Flashman, many years later.

Although I can vaguely remember the family I was too young to recall very much about them. Mr. and Mrs. Algar and their son Edwin replaced them in the house and farm.

Mrs. Algar was a short-ish lady and what we would call well developed. She always wore a wrap around style apron and didn't mix to any great extent with the rest of the ladies of the village. She was always very friendly with my family who were her next-door neighbours, probably because Ray and myself were the only friends their son had. The lad was retarded in his speech and could be a bit of an embarrassment, but he was always willing to be part of our games.

Mr. Algar was a very tall autocratic man, always dressed immaculately even when going to work on the farm. His boots and leggings were always clean and shining. Working boots and a warehouse coat were kept at the farm for changing into when he was away from the prying eyes of the villagers. I think he had received some sort of military training. He delivered milt to St Germans every morning, going from house to house with his old but immaculate Morris Light Van. The outside was painted navy blue with black mudguards and the running boards (we didn't call them wings in those days). The inside was a gleaming white and was forever being touched up with new paint, or being scrubbed.

The rear of the van was equipped with a small platform, on which stood three tall polished milk churns, with shining brass taps. The amount of milk required by each customer was drawn off into the highly polished measures hanging on a rail along the inside and transferred to the customer's jugs.

The van doubled up as a private car as was usual in those days, but there was a routine where the whole van had to be emptied before it was used. The rear floor had to be covered with mats and a thick board with padding was placed across the bodywork to act as a seat for Edwin.

Mr. Algar wasn't a particularly popular man in the village but was accepted on the same level as everyone else, if ever help was needed. He didn't really like small boys, but when you live next door to them, and you have a farm with fields that need exploring, what can you do, but recognise their existence. Sometimes...........

"He was a proper bloody Tory," was how one of his distant relatives described him recently, when we were having a discussion about the past. Why their house was built so large in the middle of the village I never found out........until many years later.

The front of the house had a large concreted canopy over the front doorway, supported by two pillars. The whole frontage was surrounded by a wrought iron fence, which enclosed a small lawn. It's still there so nothing has changed. The house is much higher than all the other houses in the village, with huge rooms that were mostly unfurnished. They did have an old piano though, kept in one of the unoccupied bedrooms, on which Edwin spent a lot of time banging on the keyboards. With a window open wide, the whole village was entertained. I don't think that in the years that I knew the family he was ever allowed outside the back garden of their house to play with other children even though only about two cars a day passed through the village.

On the other side of our house lived a branch of the Jane family. That is the name that dominated the whole village. Head of the family was Mr. Alf Jane, a jovial sort of fellow but for some reason he had lost a leg and used an artificial limb. However he was very active, and went off in his lorry every morning to the St Ive area to collect milk that the farmers had placed in churns on platforms at lorry height, at convenient spots beside the road for delivery to the Creamery at Saltash. He would deposit clean churns for the next day's collection, and swing those heavy full churns on to the back of the lorry. Thos full churns, each containing thirteen gallons of milk, were not the easiest of things to handle. They were tall tapered metal containers that were difficult to get much of a lift on, with the two handles positioned so close together. Many a swear word was uttered, sometimes loudly, when fingers or toes became trapped.

Mrs. Bessie Jane, Alf's wife was a happy soul and could see the funny side of everything. Rather large she was a typical country wife, who spent all of her time polishing and cleaning. She always seemed to be wearing little small glasses that were perched on the end of her nose, and she had a habit of looking over the top of them.

They had two daughters, Irene who was about five years older than myself and Patsy who was about a year younger. I can remember that Irene (usually called Rene) had flaming red hair, and a temper to match. To call her Ginger was to ask for trouble with a capital T. She packed a deadly punch, and wasn't afraid to demonstrate it on anyone, regardless of size. She was a big girl and many a large schoolboy at Landrake School had suffered at her hands. Patsy was more of a blonde if memory serves me correctly, and not quite such a large girl. They were both robust to say the least, but were good friends of Ray and myself. It paid us to be friends with them anyway, they had the better of the two wireless sets in the village.

The original family of the Jane's lived in the detached cottage in the centre of the village (now renamed "Forge Cottage").

The cottage was kept spotlessly clean, and there was shining brass in every nook and cranny. The floors in the downstairs rooms were large slabs of slate, over an earth base, mats and rugs covered the blue slate and helped to make the place a little warmer.

The mother of the family was known to everyone, adults and children alike, as Granny Jane. She was a very tall lady, and to me, had always been very old. Always dressed in a typical Victorian grandmother style, she would stand at the door of her porch beside the road and talk to all the children. She loved to have children around, perhaps the fact that she had several of her own made her feel lost without them. Her popularity with all the children from the area could be that she had always had a biscuit barrel that was full of "double biscuits" with sweet cream in the middle.

Some of her well-known cures for ailments didn't always meet with approval though. She recommended paraffin oil on chilblains, and for a cold a thin sliver of orange peel turned inside out in each nostril should be a certain cure. For toothaches the peel of a turnip or swede got very hot and placed behind the ear should do the trick, and give almost instant relief. A mixture of black treacle and sulphur, taken twice a day, could cure blood disorders, boils and spots. But her herb beer was not to be criticized. (It was lovely).

Her late husband started out his working life on a farm but suffered a broken leg in a farm accident. It became apparent that all did not go well with the leg and that he would not be able to carry on working on the farm. Capt Coyton the Squire heard of the problem, and built him a carpenter's shop on a piece of land next to the blacksmith's shop. Granny Jane was the daughter of that blacksmith, Henry Bennett. He occupied the blacksmith shop on the opposite side of the road from the cottage that Granny Jane lived in, hence the name of Forge Cottage, but later moved to the original forge at the top of the village.

Living at home in the cottage, when I lived in the village were Bill Jane the village carpenter, Sid Jane who worked at Holwood Quarry, and another son Herbert. He did not enjoy good health having joined the American Army before the war, and contracted T.B. He came home to live with his family and lived on a generous Pension from the U.S.A.

The only private car in the village, mentioned earlier, belonged to him. Up until 1932 he had a Morris Cowley 4 seater tourer with a "Bull Nose" radiator. When a new model came out in 1932 he changed it for a more sporty model. It was a Morris Cowley two-seater tourer with a dickey seat. Dickey seats were a little foldaway two-seater cushion and backrest, behind the driver and passenger hood, that folded down into the body when not being used. There was no protection from the weather when riding in the dickey, but what fun it was.

Mr. Herbert, as he was known to all the children in the area, was a very generous and popular gentleman. A large man who always looked a little pale, he was respected wherever he went in the area. A well dressed gent, always wearing a collar and tie, he was always willing to help, and was always on hand to take people to visit sick relatives or an emergency visit to the doctor. I think that the villagers made more use of his car than Mr. Herbert himself. Another brother was Mr. Alf Jane who we met earlier. There were two sisters who visited occasionally, one named Ethyl, but I cannot recall the seventh of the children.

In the corner house at the top of the village lived Ernest Jane. A widower, he was to my eyes always very, very old. He had a small flower garden beside the road at the end of his cottage, with a large vegetable garden at the rear of the house. If Uncle Ernest, as we insisted that he was called, was never remembered for anything else he would always be remembered for the smell of his roses. Rambling roses covered the rustic fence that surrounded the little garden, and combined with some of the well-tended roses and other flowers in the garden, it was impossible to escape the wonderful scent.

I don't think that I ever did find out with any certainty, in what way he fitted into the family, but I believe he was the brother of Granny Jane's late husband. He worked as a carpenter at Pentille Estate, and travelled to and from work every day, about six miles each way, by motorcycle. In the early days he rode an old James motorcycle with a long petrol tank and acetylene lighting. He later changed to a newer model James two-stroke with modern electric lighting.

His motorcycles were his pride and joy. At night, if the weather was fine, he would spend an hour after his evening meal, giving the machine a good clean down and a polish. Boys were allowed to watch but kept well clear. You touched the thing at your peril. After cleaning it was always covered up and put away in a lean to inside his garden gate. There was no need to lock it away in those days, no one would steal it, or damage it in any way.

For many years he had a black spaniel dog, Bruce, who took up a lot of his spare time. The dog was groomed until his coat glistened, and fed until the poor animal could eat no more. Eventually the dog was so fat that it could hardly move, but it would still follow his master around wherever he went. Many times Mr. Jane has been seen going around his garden shouting for Bruce and the poor dog was behind him trying to catch up.

Mr. Earnest was a very keen gardener and as well as his wonderful flower garden, always had plenty of produce for the Harvest Festival or to pass on to anyone who appeared to be having a hard time, either in the village or outside.

His housekeeper should go down in the history of the village as the most genial person who ever lived there. Hilda Prideaux who came from Cargreen was not an old person. I found out in later years that she was about twenty years older than me. A confirmed Old Maid she certainly enjoyed life.

She had a laugh that could be heard all over the village. She kept the little cottage spotless, and always seemed to be scrubbing the blue slate floors, until they almost shone. There was a lot of brass around the house, as seemed to be usual in those days, and most mornings would find Hilda, as she was known to everyone, sat at the end of the kitchen table surrounded by Brasso and dusters. If it wasn't brass, it was cutlery and kitchen utensils being cleaned with a pumice stone.

The stable-type door to the house was always wide open, and everyone was welcome to just walk in and have a chat. There was always a homely smell of baking around the house, and all visitors would be offered a cup of tea and either a biscuit or a currant bun.

Afternoons would see Hilda all cleaned up and wearing a clean freshly ironed apron and looking for something to do for someone else. During the summer months she would assemble a gang of children from far and wide, and take them off to have a walk across the fields or maybe pick primroses or blackberries, depending on the season.

Picnics at Pillaton Mill, beside the River Lynher were always something to look forward to. It usually ended in games that she would join in and act as if she was the same age as the children. Games that started off as being beside the river often ended up in the river. More than once she, and some of the children, came home with what can only be described as the "wet look".

Anyone who ever met with Hilda couldn't forget that loud infectious laughter and those round, rosy cheeks that always had that well scrubbed look about them. She just laughed and ate her way through life, and they both showed, laughter in her eyes, and the food everywhere else.

An interesting point about this house, situated as it is at the "T" junction at the top of the village, a road sign was erected and placed high up on the wall, just under the eves of the roof, with one finger pointing towards Tideford, and the other finger pointing towards Saltash. It said Saltash 8 ½ miles, Landrake 2 ½ miles, and the other indicated St Germans 4 ½ miles, Tideford 2 ½ miles. Exactly when this road sign was erected is a bit vague, but it does appear on photographs of the village in 1900, at a height that made the destinations clear to high horse drawn wagonette passengers. It stayed in that position for many years, and it was not lowered to a more conventional height until the early fifties. That in turn has now been replaced by a plastic covered piece of metal that glows when a light is shone on it.

Across the road in a house behind a fairly high stone wall, that encompassed a large garden as well as the house and village Church, Mr. and Mrs. Hooper lived for a year or two while I was very young. Their family were mostly grown up, except for one son Harold, about my own age. I can only remember Mr. Hooper as a very small man who worked on the farm at Holwood, as did the grown up sons. Mrs. Hooper was endowed with what I suppose would be called a fuller figure, but with a very high pitched voice. My, how she could screech at those boys in her family.

As they all seemed to be smokers they applied for a licence to sell tobacco, and eventually sold cigarettes from their front door. There was a little sign over the doorway at the front porch. H.HOOPER, LICENSED TO SELL TOBACCO.

To get fathers "Baccy" I always went to the back door. Just in case Mr. Berryman the policeman happened to come along at the wrong time.

The family moved away to seek their fortunes at a farm near Totnes in Devon. The house was then occupied by another member of the Jane family. This was to be Mr. Charles Jane and his wife Annie.

They brought with them Mrs. Jane's sister who was a permanent invalid and spent her life looking out of her bedroom window and either doing embroidery or reading. Her huge family Bible was her first choice of reading matter. Uncle Charlie as he was known, was a Gamekeeper at Holwood, and had previously lived in a little remote cottage at the edge of the woods. I had been to that cottage many times, and received many lessons on wildlife from Uncle Charlie. Although his job meant that he had to take a very balanced look at all wild life, he would only destroy vermin.

He had a row of boxes and cages under the hedge at the side of his cottage, where injured animals and birds were nursed back to health. There were always an odd pheasant or hedgehog receiving some care in those boxes.

The cottage was situated in a large depression in the land, and was sheltered from strong winds. Along one hedge of the garden was a row of beehives, always full of bees. The clover from the surrounding fields and the numerous flowers that were always a feature of the south facing garden, gave the bees an abundant supply of pollen to make into honey. The bees didn't have far to travel, and the still air made their task fairly easy. One of Charlie's greatest joys was his garden. There were always plenty of vegetables to pass around to friends, and I cannot remember ever going to their cottage when there were no flowers on the polished table in front of the living room window. A slightly built man with a walrus moustache, with weather beaten face and arms the colour of mahogany, Charlie was always busy.

His wife, Aunt Annie, was a very small lady, who shared her husband's love of the wild life that was just outside their door. The cottage was too far off the beaten track for any tradesmen to call. Aunt Annie had to arrange to be in the village when the butcher or grocer came, or rely on someone else to get what she wanted.

Her sister, known as Miss Lizzie, despite her handicap was a very happy person, but lonely. She loved to have children or anyone else visit her in her room, where she would talk about a wide range of subjects. An amazing lady she saw beauty in a everything, even the rain, although she admitted that she might have had a different view if she was out in it. When she moved to the village from the cottage, she was taken away from her greatest joy, that of being able to look out of her window at any time of the day or night and watch her birds and animals in their natural habitat. She loved to watch badgers. While Charlie was paid to destroy them it was not unknown for him to place any young that he found in a distressed condition in a position where they would stand a good chance of being found by the adult badgers. Miss Lizzie did admit though that she soon found out that the folk of the village more than made up for the animals that she had missed.

The only house that I haven't mentioned is the house built around 1922 on a high piece of land on the Saltash road, opposite the entrance to Wisewandra. Beside the small white-framed gate, with black iron decorative bars, was a wider gate of the same design, with Pinglestone Villa painted on a varnished board. Inside the gates were wide, gravel-covered paths, wide enough to enable a car to drive around the central flower garden. This was a novelty in those days, very few people had the room for such an ornamental drive, and fewer still had the cars to drive on it.

Mr. Greet, a retired farmer and his wife who had previously farmed at Wisewandra, had no car, but they were probably thinking along such lines when they built the house. It was a bit grand for the area, with red tiles on the roof, and lots of white painted Bay windows.

CHAPTER 3 – THE CHAPEL

The most important building in the village was the Chapel at the lower end of the village. Most of the village activities were centred on the Chapel and took place either within the Chapel or in the Sunday School room at the rear. There were no Community Centres in those days, so the best use was made of the available space. In the Parish of Quethiock there were two little nonconformist Chapels, one in the village of Quethiock and the other at Blunts.

Before the building of the Chapels there was a licensed nonconformist meeting house at the home of a Mr. Samuel Tay in the village of Quethiock, followed shortly after by a license being granted for meetings to be held in the kitchen of the farm at Wisewandra, the farm adjoining Blunts on the Saltash road.

In 1839 a small Chapel was built at Quethiock to look after the needs of the villagers, whilst at Blunts, land was donated by a Mr. Snell for a small Chapel to be built. The local parishioners donated the materials and labour and in 1843 the new Chapel was completed. An extension was added within the next few years in the form of a stable to accommodate the ponies of visiting preachers, who travelled many miles to take Sunday service in the remote villages. Above the stables the Sunday School was built and divided from the Chapel by a varnished wooden partition, which was removed to turn the Sunday School into a Gallery when the Chapel needed extra seating.

The exterior of the Chapel remains today, with very few alterations from when it was built. The outside walls were cement rendered early in the twentieth century, but nothing else changed. The original stone inserted in the wall near the entrance still bears the chiselled inscription "1843". The original entrance was converted into a window and a new entrance door and doorway made before the turn of the century. It was with much pride that Mr. Delbridge who at the time of my youth farmed at Wisewandra and was a regular worshiper at Blunts Chapel, would give me and other boys a potted history of the Wesleyan and Methodist growth in the district. How to the licensed meeting places, part time preachers came on Sunday mornings and evenings to pass on the Good Word. Some of those preachers walked or rode their horses many miles to attend their congregations, which could on occasions be very small. Mr. Delbridge told how, in the early Nineteenth Century the Church of England as we know it today was in a state of decline throughout Cornwall, and in this area in particular.

In 1836 the Methodist Conference had decided to ordain its own Ministers, who, after training and Examination (mostly oral), and accepting the doctrines of Wesley's "Sermons" and "Notes on the New Testament" would be sent out as travelling Preachers. Soon Wesleyan Methodist Chapels were springing up all over Cornwall. The two Chapels of Quethiock and Blunts were to follow and with the attached Sunday Schools were well attended. There were very few children in the parish that did not attend Sunday School regardless of the religion of the parents.

The Chapel was built originally by the Bible Christians, who could not afford the upkeep, so the Chapel was passed to the Wesleyans.

It was recorded that the fiftieth anniversary of Blunts Chapel was celebrated in great style with a large crowd gathering in the evening. The main event would appear to be the first reading of a poem, specially written by a Mr. Tobias Higman of Brightor, near Landrake, and running into some thirty six verses, recording the history of the Chapel to that date. (See Appendix A for the full 36 verses). At one period during my attendance at the Sunday School I was expected to learn the whole poem by heart, but now I can only remember two verses.

Tobias Higman was man of words, who wrote a number of Hymns and essays. His sister Georgina was married to John Billing. There were my mother's parents. Over the years, although the outside appearance has remained much the same as when it was first built, the interior has seen some alterations. Lower backed pews with no doors have replaced the original high-backed pews with their side doors to the central aisles. Exactly when I cannot trace but there were still a few pews with doors during my early days. On the shelf at the front of all the pews was a small brass frame that held the name of the family who had reserved that pew by making regular payments for the rent of the family pews. The Searl family from Furslowe Farm had the front pew on the left side of the aisle, with the Tucker family from Molenic behind them, and the third pew was

When I was a small boy I can vividly recall a Mr. Davey of St Ive spending a lot of time wire brushing the whole outside of the Chapel to removed all the mosses and lichen that had grown over the cement covered walls. When all was ready the whole building was painted a light grey colour. There were imitation blocks on the walls, created by light impressions being made in the cement. When the repainting was carried out I somehow felt a little let down by discovering that the huge concrete blocks were after all only drawn in with a flat pencil, of the type used by carpenters. But the whole thing did look very smart until my cousin Bernard from Trebrown replaced the funny face that he had previously drawn on the end of the stable. I don't think that face was ever completely removed again for many years. I did notice on my visit this year that the outside is now roughcast but still coloured light grey.

During my days in the village the whole building was kept clean by Mrs. Wythe, the wife of the village postman. They lived in the house next to the Chapel, and spent many hours cleaning and polishing.

Their little cottage was condemned after the death of Mr. and Mrs. Wythe, and was purchased by the Chapel in 1961 for the Sum of £50 plus £20 Solicitor's fees. The interior walls were removed by voluntary labour and the roof lowered to make a useful additional room. A doorway was opened up beside the pulpit to make a direct access to the new room.

The huge brass oil lamps that hung from the ceiling providing light for evening Services, would sparkle like a million dollars when lit. They gave out a lovely soft yellow glow but not without the occasional paraffin smell when the doors were opened and a draught made the flame flicker that little bit more than usual.

The lamps were obviously not new, there was the odd dent, and signs of repair by soldering where leaks developed over the years. Any repairs would probably have been carried out by Bill Jane, or possibly his father, as they were strong supporters of the Chapel, and self appointed handymen.

The Chapel Account Book shows that they were bought in 1901 at a cost of £5.7s.0d. The money was raised by a Public Tea and Service, from which the collection and some donations by members were added to the Harvest Festival profits.

Heating was by two large Valor paraffin heaters, that when lit made magic lantern style patterns on the ceiling with the light from the flame passing through the different shaped holes in the top, that were designed to allow the heat to escape. Although they were capable of taking the chill off the building, it must be admitted that it did not get too hot, and there was a smell of paraffin.

I was introduced to the Sunday School when I was about three years old. I was sent off in best clothes with hair brushed and shoes cleaned to join the rest of the children from the adjoining farms and hamlets, to be ushered up those concrete steps to the room above the stable. Rather steep steps I seem to recall, with high risers, which stretched young legs to their limit. Here, our Star Cards would be collected on entry, to be stamped with a little blue star to record our attendance. These cards would be handed back as we went home, and not before under any circumstances. I wonder why? Those Stars were important. The number of Stars decided the size of the reward when it came around to Prize Giving time. It would be most embarrassing, living only three doors away from the Sunday School, to be rewarded for attendance by only a decorated card on which was written a short Biblical text, instead of a good story book.

Sunday School was always conducted during my years there, by Mr. Searl of Furslow Farm. I can only ever remember him as a slightly stooping man with a white moustache, highly polished boots and leather leggings. Every Sunday afternoon he would walk the mile and a half from Furslow to reach Blunts at exactly the right time, 2.30pm. With him would be his two daughters Maude and Winifred, who would take it in turns to play the little harmonium organ while we children made noises that passed for singing. Another of Mr. Searl's daughters was only a couple of years older than myself, and didn't turn up so regularly in the early days. As we got a little older it became the custom for all the boys to loiter outside the Chapel, until Mr. Searl arrived and wait for him to say as he passed, "Come on boys......... Times up". Then we would all pass along beside the black painted railings, and up those steps to the Sunday School for an hour. There was normally a good attendance at the Sunday School. Gerald, Gordon, Betty, Mona and Mary Gimblett, Molly Lansley and her sister Daisy, Eustace Holman from Clapper Bridge, Jan and Nancy Doney from Holwood, three of the Hoard children from Holwood, are just some of the names I can recall.

Without exception the highlight of the year must have been the Sunday School Anniversary. There would be weeks of the regular Sunday School being given over to learning new Hymns and tunes. Everyone had to be word perfect, and probably the biggest task was we all had to learn to sing in tune at the same time as an organist that was not really sure of the tune anyway.

Our greatest fear, as pupils, was that we might get singled out to sing a solo, or something equally embarrassing. So it was not in our best interest to do too good a job, or let it be known how good you could sing (if you could sing), until all the soloists had been sorted out.

There was always a midweek practice when the adult members of the Chapel who were going to sing at the Anniversary, would join us and add to the confusion. We didn't always have the same organist, some guest organists played at a different speed, some didn't even read music, (or so the stories are told). Some female voices were a little overpowering and out of tune with everyone else, but eventually it would all fall into an acceptable place.

As anniversary day drew closer all the mothers of the area were busy making new clothes for themselves and daughters, and helping out those who couldn't sew or didn't possess a sewing machine. There was a certain amount of secrecy about the whole thing. Anniversary time was to be the highlight of the year, and you didn't really want everyone to know what you were going to wear on such an occasion. Boys also were expected to turn out in new clothes, maybe a new suit, or at least a new shirt and for the more adventurous, a new tie. It was usual that boys clothes were bought or made a "little on the big side, to grow into". Jacket sleeves were turned up at the cuffs, and trousers were turned up at the bottom for the first year's wear "for best", and then let down for the next year for School.

It was normally the time of the year when new boots (no shoes in those days when you were of school age) were bought for boys, which would last for at least a whole year and then probably be passed on.

For days before the Sunday service there would be much activity within the Chapel building. The pulpit end of the Chapel would be transformed by building a platform around the sides and to the front of the pulpit to accommodate all the singers. This was achieved by the use of surplus seating forms placed upon trestles especially made and kept for the purpose.

This was the occasion when the men of the village and beyond came to do their bit for the community. The trestles and forms obviously didn't always go together in the same position every year, so there was the occasional bit of wobbling of the structure. Odd bits of wood were always in demand to rectify large discrepancies, but small adjustments could usually be made by "trigging" up with a Star or Gold Flake fag packet, suitably folded.

A central set of wooden steps were erected from the aisle to the platform and securely fastened, at least in later years. There was one occasion when one side of the steps became detached and all the singers were marooned on the platform, while Bill Jane the village carpenter went off to get some extra wood and nails to make the structure safe.

The Sunday morning Service was usually attended by the normal congregation plus a few extras from around the district, but all the Sunday School pupils were expected to attend. The whole service was used as a kind of unofficial dress rehearsal, when nervous young voices made their first public performance of their singing voices and their capacity or otherwise, to remember words and tunes would be demonstrated.

And be commented on afterwards! There were occasions when substitutes had to be hurriedly made when stage fright took over.

The afternoon Service was the major attraction. The Sunday School partition would be removed and extra seating provided by forms in the balcony to meet the needs of the visiting congregation. It was usual for chairs from village houses to be brought in and placed in the aisle or any other space where there was room. It was a sign of poor attendance if this did not happen.

To this great occasion would come too the adult singers who had only attended the first practice, and who were not aware of the many alterations that had taken place since first sight of the Hymn sheet. Some verses would be omitted for a variety of reasons, and words that were difficult to say were changed if possible.

Over the years there were many red faces, and I assume many a prayer for the platform to open up to hide the embarrassment caused by singing the wrong verse, tune or words. Every year we knew which ladies were going to demonstrate a voice that had not been heard at rehearsals.

Children had every reason for being in attendance at this Service. Piled high beside the preacher would be those awards for attendance. The Sunday School Secretary would be hovering nearby, just in case of problems pronouncing some of the names. There was always a lot of speculation as to who was going to get those big books that always seemed to be at the bottom of the pile. There were small books too. Who was going to get them?

The names of the prize winners and the trip to the front to receive your award was timed just before the sermon, and all those dreary speeches and reports about what had happened in the previous year. I suppose previous experience had shown that there was not much enthusiasm for singing for a while after receiving a new book.

I can still remember the first award that I received. Inside the front cover was the illustrated label that said that the book was awarded for attendance in the year 1928 – 1929. The book had the exciting title of People of the Chasm. Not that I could read it. I hadn't even started School. Eventually I did read it and kept that book for many years.

Not many children were expected to attend the Sunday night Service as it meant a long walk home for most of them, but there was usually a good adult congregation, with a special preacher for the occasion.

Wednesday was the day that the children had their best day with a special tea party in the afternoon, before the evening Service. For the children of school age there was the added attraction of leaving school early to allow time to get home and prepare for the sports and games that usually preceded the tea.

On the opposite side of the road from the Chapel was the path field known as Bladders (no-one seems to know why) that led to Holwood Farm and all the farm cottages. It was not just a normal footpath, but a wide track across three fields, with wide gates to allow wagons to pass through. Weather permitting, games were held here and the wide, grass covered track across the field was an excellent place for cricket or football. The track in addition to being wide, was straight and fairly smooth, so it made a good spot for races. Some parents were not quite so sure that games were a good thing before the evening service. There was the occasional accident to new clothes, or to the wearer.

Tea was always an elaborate affair, held in the school room, with trestle tables laden down with fancy cakes, jellies and sandwiches, washed down with gallons of home made lemonade or fizzy drinks. On occasions, this was also known to take its toll on the junior attendance at the evening performance.

Things didn't always go as planned. I can recall that on one occasion a visiting preacher at the Wednesday evening service, whilst delivering a particular pulpit-thumping sermon, collapsed and died. Fortunately incidents of this nature were very rare. This incident did give the villagers a new topic of conversation for a few days, and a report did appear in the Cornish Times the following Friday. The village didn't get its name in the press very often.

There was always one thing that as a small boy I could never understand. Why did all the children get a thin paper hymn sheet that was expected to survive being stuffed into pockets and used two or three times a week for several weeks? The adults were given sheets with music on them. They had good handbags to carry the sheets in, and if they turned up for a practice without a sheet, there was always a replacement available. Even small boys could see the unfairness that existed in this world.

Throughout the year various Concerts and Musical evenings would take place in the Chapel with varying degrees of success. A very popular visitor, who would entertain with a wide variety of songs, both light hearted and serious, was Mr. John Payne, a huge negro singer who had sung and acted as a stand-in to the great Paul Robson. John Payne had made his home near Liskeard, and was in great demand throughout the district.

The Sunday School was on occasions, turned into the village Concert

Hall for visits from such organisations as the Landrake Concert Party, who featured the Landrake Handbell Ringers under the direction of Mr. Enis Barrett. Mr. Barrett earned his living as a Council roadman, and travelled around the district on a little Francis Barnet two-stroke motorcycle. An elderly gentleman with white hair and moustache, and a few very brown teeth, but it must be admitted that he did organise his ringers to produce some very pleasant music. The Concert party also included a rather large lady, (whose name I cannot remember) who gave hilarious readings from Jan Stewar at least twice during the evening. There was also a gent that always sung a song entitled "In the Back Seat of a little Austin Seven" and would always make up a few verses of his own to add to the original version.

Whilst these Concerts would take place in the Sunday School room, there would be a great deal of Primus pumping below stairs in the stable, to heat water to make tea for refreshments. Tea was then carried up the stairs in huge copper teapots that would have been given a special polish for the occasion. It was tea or nothing to quench your thirst, the only coffee available those days was Camp Coffee in bottles, and considered too expensive to give away, without adding to the admission price. Soft drinks were only available during the summer months when the Corona lorry came around. At that time the year there were no Concerts anyway.

Harvest Festival would come later in the year, and was celebrated with much effort and hard work by everyone in the area. Produce from fields and gardens would be placed around the front of the Chapel almost concealing the pulpit. Large trays of highly polished red apples would be displayed alongside champion sized marrows. Decorated baskets of fruit and jars of honey would jostle for a space beside specimen displays of potatoes that would be a credit at any agricultural show.

Reputations as gardeners and preserve makers were at stake here, with a wonderful chance to show off personal one-up-man-ship very discreetly. Although village life was one of help your neighbour, if there was a chance to prove your superiority in some way you grabbed that chance, no matter where it presented itself.

Along the front step would be a section reserved for produce produced from children's gardens, but that was usually filled with flowers from Mum's flower garden. It wasn't always your own Mum's garden either........ but there were no rules to say otherwise.

The centre section in front of the pulpit was filled with a model rick of corn, made with three different types of corn and perfectly thatched. This had been made many years previously by Mr. Jane, the father of the village carpenter, who had also been the previous village carpenter during his lifetime. Behind the pulpit attached to the wall was a hand painted and carved scroll stating that "The God of the Harvest Is Our God". In the centre of this scroll was a carved Harvest Sheaf. There were a few occasions when the Sheaf was hidden by a printed notice to say that it had been donated. Perhaps it was to encourage a little extra trade to come his way.

The scroll and wooden sheaf were hand made by Mr. Earnest Jane, in memory of his wife. There was a small inscription that read "Presented to the Chapel in Memory of Mary Ann Jane who died Feb 8th 1926. From her Husband and Family". Full sheaves of corn were brought in, along with all the best fruit and vegetables. Every household was expected to make a contribution in some form.

The two Sunday services were always well attended, even to the state of requiring extra seating for the evening service. Traditional harvest hymns were sung with great gusto, being lively tunes that everyone knew. "Bringing in the Sheaves" and "We Plough the Fields and Scatter", that even farmers and farm workers who were not normally seen inside the Chapel at other times of the year, would join in. The following Wednesday nigh there would be the traditional Harvest Supper when once more the Sunday School would be transformed into a large dining room. There would be trestle tables the full length of the room with what we now term the "top table"

There was always a plentiful supply of homemade cakes, sandwiches, and goodies supplied by the ladies of the village and surrounding farms. After the tables were cleared of food and drink the tables were packed away, with the exception of the two or three which would be required later, to place the produce to be sold on. Forms, which had been used for seating during the supper, would be arranged to provide extra seating for the evening service, when the wooden partition between schoolroom and chapel would be once more removed. The day's activities would end with the produce from the pulpit area being transferred to the Sunday School, and auctioned. By today's standards I suppose it was all very quiet and not very exciting, but everything was organised by a very few stalwarts of the Chapel, and everyone seemed to enjoy themselves in their own modest way.

During the summer a trip was always organised to the seaside for the Sunday School pupils and such members of their families who wanted to go. This usually meant just children and mothers with just the odd couple of men who were connected with the Sunday School and Chapel in some way. In my day the horse and wagonette trips to the seaside had passed, but only just. There had only been two or three visits to the seaside by motor charabanc before I went on my first trip.

We were now in the age of the charabanc, usually supplied by one of two local firms, Deebles of Upton Cross, or Truscotts of Rilla Mill. Early on the appointed day we would all congregate at the top of the village, armed with bags containing towels, bathing costumes and sandwiches for the day.

Thermos flasks of tea were taken to cater for the needs of the adults, but not for the children. This was the day when we could get a treat, in the form of a bottle of some new type of drink. The Corona man brought lemonade and orangeade, maybe even dandelion and burdock if he hadn't sold out in one of the larger villages before reaching our little hamlet. Today we would be able to sample such things as Vimto, Ice cream Soda, and other brightly coloured liquids on offer at the seaside.

The busses themselves looked to our eyes in the late 1920s and early 1930s the height of luxury. They were in reality fairly old vehicles and not very reliable. Most of the charabancs of that period were ex Army lorries, with special bodies built on them. In some cases the bodies were interchangeable with lorry bodies so that they were always at work. Passenger carrying bodies would replace lorry bodies on the night before a trip.

The two coaches supplied by Deebles were Crossley 14 H. P. ex R.A.F tenders, with the wonderful names of Eddystone Belle and The Bluebird. One body was made by Mumfords Bodyworks of Plymouth and one was made by Mr. Deeble Senior, with the assistance of the carpenter of Darley Ford, a Mr. Showell. These bodies were the very latest design, with doors all along the left hand side, one door to each row of seats. At the end of each trip the seats were all removed and the bodies reverted to the role of delivering coal in sacks. The doors made for easy loading and unloading. These were in use between 1927 and 1932 I am informed. The first year or two that I went on these trips, it was in one of these, the original old type charabancs, with a canvas hood that was folded down during the summer, and detachable side screens to keep the wind out.

The coaches did improve though. Fully coach-built bodies became available after a few years, with an aisle the full length of the coach. This was not all good news, it meant that boys on the back seat, or anywhere else, were within reach of parents, who were always willing to hand out punishment, to curb the high spirits of boys – even on a day out.

Reliability of the coaches didn't seem to improve much. There were occasions when we were very late leaving for our day out, due to some minor breakdown. A can of petrol was always carried on the side, as petrol stations were few and far between. A supply of water had to be carried too, boiling radiators were a regular occurrence, and seemed to be the one thing that could be relied upon to heighten the day's excitement for the boys.

The day trip was normally to Looe, the nearest seaside that could be reached and give a reasonable time at the resort. One year a fierce argument raged for several weeks while the powers that decided such events considered more exciting things.

Polzeath was considered to be a place that would be a good day out, away from the crowds. Fierce arguments raged, but eventually a decision was reached. The final destination was to be Polzeath, but for that year only as an experiment.

The bus broke down on the outward journey and we were very late getting there. When we did arrive, there was a tearoom, and an Ice Cream hut, and that was it. There were a few houses along the coast but well back from the shore. No fishing boats, nowhere to fish from and nowhere to even buy a fishing line. North Cornwall winds are always cold and didn't they blow that day. There was nowhere to shelter from the winds and nothing to pass away the time but sit in the bus with all those dreary adults who had arranged the whole day out. The sea was far too rough for children. Even adults were reluctant to venture in the foaming surf. Rain forced an earlier than usual return trip home, but there was a little compensation. When we arrived on the outskirts of Bodmin we stopped in a long line of cars and buses full of day-trippers at a Fish and Chip shop.

This was a rarity indeed, not many of us saw such a thing during the rest of the year. To be able to go into the shop with a shiny sixpence clutched firmly in your hand, and come out with a bag of hot, freshly fried fish and chips was heaven. The wonderful aroma of vinegar and salt on that hot, steaming delicacy must be every boy's dream at the end of a day out. Even the newspaper that it was wrapped in would probably have some interesting items of news that had not been seen before. With luck you might even get the cartoon section.

To be able to sit in the bus and eat them all without having to share with the rest of the family was pure joy. When we had fish and chips on our trips to Looe, parents always seemed to find an excuse to slip off, and then come back with the chips already divided up and in separate bits of greaseproof paper. There were generally excuses about why there was no fish, or at least, why the portion was so small.

We never did go to Polzeath again. After that our day trips were confined to Looe. It did have a lot of advantages. It didn't take too long to get there normally, and there was always plenty to do when you arrived. The sands were safe and soft, plenty of rocks and rock pools that would become full of small fish and crabs when the tide came in.

There was always the town to explore when the beach became

crowded, as everyone moved back to escape the incoming tide. There were fishing boats too tied up along the Quay that always had something interesting going on.

As a bonus, there were some very tempting cliffs to climb and explore. From the top of these it looked as if you could see for miles, but in reality it was only a couple of miles. After all, the cliffs were only about forty feet high, but it seemed a long way up to young eyes. All along the rear of the sands there were cliffs that gave a fellow a feeling of adventure, without getting too involved and having to shout for help if the going got touch. At the top there was a quite good road leading back to the beach if the downward trip seemed a little daunting.

Little shops selling shells and the usual seaside gifts all helped to make the enforced walk around the narrow crowded streets less of a boring experience. There must have been quite a number of shops selling ice cream. Judging by the number of people going around eating them but we didn't seem to find them very often. I could never quite understand why every shop in the town had to be visited, when the fishing line a fellow needed was for sale in the shop on the sea front, only yards from where we had been sitting. To a young lad much valuable time was wasted looking at knitting patterns, lace, ribbons and such trial items that would not be bought today, but talked about for weeks to come.

In the early days a visit to the Looe Rabbitries was a must. This was a large warehouse that had five or six floors, full of caged rabbits of every colour and description. It was always sweltering hot in the seemingly windowless building. There never seemed to be much in the way of ventilation, and it wasn't the most pleasant smelling place around. The rabbits took the blame. It was always crowded with visitors admiring the poor fluffy animals that would spend their brief lives caged in this hellhole, to be admired and then ordered and made into a pair of gloves or a pair of slippers.

There was always a plentiful supply of rabbit skin goods on sale in the shop on the ground floor, and there appeared to be no shortage of customers. In later years the operation was scaled down and the rabbits were only kept as exhibition animals which customers would be willing to pay to see. Over the years there had been many protests about the conditions, from visitors and the local population.

But a day out at the seaside was supposed to be centred on the sea. The day would not be complete without watching the steamer come in. Every afternoon all eyes would be on the horizon to catch a first glance of what, to our eyes, was the huge ocean going liner, just like the ones in the picture books. It would come in quite close to shore to be met by dozens of small boats and tenders, to bring passengers ashore. They would be landed on the steps that were built on the harbour side of the Banjo Pier. Seemingly hundreds of them. The passengers had been picked up earlier, usually at Plymouth and had a choice of three or four destination points along the coast, where passengers would disembark for an hour or two to spend time on the beach or just stroll around the streets.

To those of us who were used to the county life, some of the people we saw were dressed very unusual. A lot of the young men had striped jackets and white boaters. The young ladies had thin dresses that blew in the wind and wide hats that always seemed to be blowing off. It was a bit like looking at those advertisements in the paper, coming alive. It certainly made our clothing look very dull. Young men who came with us, all dressed in their best flannel trousers and thick sports coats, didn't look quite so smart in comparison.

The steamer would move off to the next resort further down the coast, only to return again later in the afternoon to collect its cargo of passengers that had been discharged earlier. Once more all the little boats would be busy, ferrying the passengers back to their floating palace.

The centre of attraction for the hundreds of people on the beach and along the cliffs would be the shining black, white and red vessel that seemed to be offering some sort of escape for the lucky ones.

With hindsight, and remembering the overheard conversations, I suppose the sight of these seemingly better off people, with all their finery and carefree lifestyle must have sown the first seeds of envy, and the determination to find a different way of life for many of the young people, whose life seemed to be confined to the low paid and hard work on the land. There was always much interest as the steamer turned to leave. Without exception the extra waves that were caused by the turning screws always caught a few of the small boats that were between ship and shore in an off guarded moment. Many a visitor had to travel home in a wet suit at the end of the day. Someone else's misfortune always seemed to be the cause of much handclapping and cheering.

The Banjo Pier was the point where most of the adults would go for a short walk and see the young fishermen with rod and line get their lines caught up in the propellers of the motor boats that were on hire. If Mr. Ed Doney of Holwood came on our trip he could usually be persuaded to take a few boys out for a trip around the harbour.

After the grown ups had sampled a tray of tea from the little shop on the cliffs, we would head for the bus in the car park on the quay, near the Bridge, stopping to get a bag of chips on the way. The fishing boats tied up along the side of the car park always gave us a kind of last chance to see the things that we had missed earlier, along with a last chance to get that unknown substance on your best shirt.

The organisers would count all the heads and most times a search would have to be carried out to find the people who had either got lost or whose watch had stopped. When everyone had assembled was the moment someone would realise that something had been left behind and there would be a dash to a café or shop where the wayward article may or may not have been left.

The steep hill out of Looe did, on occasions, require at least some of the passengers to get out and lend a shoulder to assist the bus. Busses were not overpowered and would manage perfectly well in areas where there were not too many steep hills, but to get out of Looe from an almost standing start, with probably a slow moving vehicle in front was not what was intended by the makers.

At the end of the day we would get back to Blunts tired and often with a bright red look that would be more painful the next day. Ponies and traps were laid on to help people home if the trip had not got back on time. This was normally the last major event of the chapel for the year.

Sunday services were of course held at eleven o clock in the mornings and at six thirty in the evenings. After about six years old I had to go to the morning service on occasions when my mother thought that the preacher would teach me something that might do me good. There was a form of compensation in that Mr. Delbridge of Wisewandra who I mentioned earlier would always find a sweet or two in his waistcoat pocket for any children that attended.

The Preacher always had Sunday dinner supplied by a nearby farm or household. From what I can remember Mr. Delbridge seemed to supply more than his fare share of Sunday dinners. (Lunches were mid morning snacks then). This was typical of the Delbridge family. The family were always at the forefront of all that was going on in the Chapel. They had a pew reserved too, with their name in that little brass frame on the shelf.

I seem to remember Mr. Delbridge as a rather short man that always seemed to be wearing a brown suit, with a gold watch chain across the front of his waistcoat, with the centre of the chain attached to a button hole with the usually bar, and a small model gold compass swinging from the centre. A little Hitler type moustache gave the appearance of a rather well off "gentleman farmer". The family either walked to chapel, or came in the well turned out pony and jingle that was their normal transport. Mr. Delbridge always had time to talk to the young people and would answer any questions they might ask. Nothing was too much trouble.

I cannot recall many visiting preachers using the stable provided to shelter their horses. There was one who was a friend of the Libby family who came on a couple of occasions, but by the late twenties and early thirties most preachers arrived by bicycle or motorcycle. These were sometimes put in the stable to keep the seats dry. There was no need to put them away for security in those days, things remained where you left them. It would bring shame on the whole village if something was stolen from a visitor.

Mr. Wythe the caretaker's husband was not to keen on some motorcycles being parked in the stable. Some left a pool of oil behind and he had the job of cleaning it up. There was a small area of waste ground on the opposite side of the road, beside the large gate to the field, where he would direct them to.

CHAPTER 4 – AND THE CHURCH

The small Mission Church (St Petrocs) was built at the turn of the century by Squire William Coryton, the Squire of Quethiock Parish, in memory of his wife Charlotte. It was a wooden framed corrugated iron building built behind a wall between a dwelling house and the blacksmiths shop. There was no belfry as we understand it but just a wooden frame holding a bell just above the roof with a small wooden cover over the top. The Church was lined with tongue and grooved wood, which I remember to be varnished. It was sparsely furnished with only about a dozen school-type chairs for seating. The only lighting available right up to the day that the Church was dismantled in 1976 were the three paraffin lamps installed when the Church was built. The floor was just bare boards, no covering of any kind.

The villagers as a whole were loyal to the Wesleyan chapel, and although there were no words ever spoken against the Church, no one ever attended a service there.

Every Sunday afternoon the Vicar of St Hughes Church of Quethiock would arrive in his old Trojan Tourer car, complete with his organist and two people to form the congregation. The Rev Lintall would act as bell ringer and spend a few minutes pulling the thin rope that tolled the solitary bell. It had a kind of thin school bell sound. Not a bit like the peal of the six bells in Pillaton Church, that could be heard ringing across the Lynher valley when it was a still Sunday morning or evening. No traffic noise to drown the far away bells in those days.

The Reverend gentleman would then hold a full Service with the organist at the very old harmonium and the two other ladies that had come with the vicar in his car. Although, as a boy I didn't give much thought to it at the time, it must have been very humiliating and soul destroying for him to do this every week.

Rev Lintell was a well-meaning man and held in high esteem in his own village. He would always speak to boys caught using the small church porch as a shelter, or whatever boys use small places for, but it would always be a friendly gesture. He was a very tall slim man with what we always referred to as a "monk's haircut" – the type with a large hole in the middle.

At the end of every Service, the last job the Vicar would do was to shut and latch the little gate that guarded the front of the porch. The porch itself was only about three feet square, and was only protected from straying dogs and passing boys by the little gate. The little brown painted structure was panelled at the lower half with a pair of crossed timbers inside a square forming the upper half. I can remember that it was very difficult to partially lift the gate to securely close and latch the gate, but no trouble to open it.

Rev Lintel's car distinguished him in the area. Trojans were rather curious cars, with a flat twin cylinder, two-stroke engine under the seat that was started by a pulling handle inside the car. Their distinctive noise, the very high fabric roof, and the solid-tyred disc wheels made it stand out among motors of the day. The car was chain driven from an epicyclic gearbox, to a direct drive rear axle.

With no differential it was difficult to steer around corners. A novelty of the car was that you could stand by the side of the car, work the gear lever to and fro, and the car would carry out the movements as you dictated, very impressive for circus use.

As it was the only car that the Church Times allowed to be advertised, it became known as the Parsons Car, or a Gods Chariot. It was said that it was the power of prayer that made these cars capable of being driven at all, more than anything else. However they were very cheap to buy and run, and extremely reliable. The difficulty in getting around corners with the car was said to be inbuilt – to help keep you on the straight and narrow path.

As if to add something to the Trojans being a parson's car, who were in those days very much against the "Demon Drink", the makers, Trojan Motor Company, were owned by Brooke Bond Tea Company.

CHAPTER 5 – HOME SWEET HOME

The house we lived in was really a semi detached, except that it was joined to the large house mentioned earlier by a loft over a passageway. A door with two small panes of glass near the top led from the road to our back door and garden. The passage was shared by the neighbours who always seemed to forget to shut the door, when the wind was in the wrong direction, which it usually was. That door would keep banging. It always seemed to be my turn to go and shut it properly. The front door also opened off the road and entered directly into the "front room" that was only used on special occasions.

Between the road and these doors was a small patch of ground that had at some time been covered by pebbles set in cement. If ever there were a day when Ray or myself complained that there was nothing to do, mother would find some kind of scraper for us to scrape off the moss that was always growing between those pebbles. We didn't complain very often.

Against the right hand wall of the front room, stood the glass cupboard that mother proudly displayed all her best bits of china, and the Present from Worcester type of ornament. The three-piece suite was rarely used, and the fire rarely lit. I can still remember that oak block pattern lino on the floor, with a few rugs scattered around, and how cold that floor was, if you stood on it with bare feet. The scullery led off from the front room. Well it was more than just a scullery; it doubled up as a dairy, with a slate bench half way along on one side. In here all the work seemed to take place. It held the meat safe, a wooden framed type of box covered in perforated zinc that stored all the type of food that we now keep in the fridge. A built in pantry stored all the other food. The slate bench gave way to a stout wooden bench half way along the side, which aced as a workbench where all the preparation of meals was carried out. Underneath at one end was a space covered with a curtain, where two buckets of drinking water were kept. A brown pitcher with a yellow rim was kept on the top to be used only to dip the water out of the buckets into kettles or wherever it was needed. There was a window over this end of the bench that opened out near the back door of Alf and Bessie Jane's house.

From spots such as this all the local news and gossip was exchanged. A short bench at the end was reserved for such rotten jobs as washing in cold water and father having a shave. He always shaved with a cutthroat razor that had to be stropped and honed on the two different types of leather strap hung together beside the bench.

Safety razors were not often used in those days, and very rarely in country areas. There was the problem of having to find a shop that stocked the replacement blades when they were needed. And they cost money. Ever Ready was the safety razor mostly used, with its single edge for shaving, and a reinforcing piece of steel on the other edge. It made a useful instrument for model makers and removing stitches from clothes that had to be altered, after its useful service as a razor. The other razor that was at all well known was the Rolls. That had a single edge blade that was rarely renewed. Before every shave the razor had to be stropped on the two grades of leather inserted in top and bottom of the heavy chrome case that the whole instrument came in. Mr. Herbert had one of these, and the sound of his blade sharpening could be heard all over the village. There was a loud click... clack... as the blade turned over when the blade handle was moved up and down the casing. I always remember Father finishing off his shave by rubbing on his block of "alum", (no after shave then), that he used to keep in a gold coloured tin, a legacy from the war. (In 1914 Princess Mary sent tobacco and a Christmas Card from her Christmas Fund to all the troops serving abroad).

All washing had to be undertaken in an enamel bowl, waste water being deposited in a bucket and then thrown away outside, usually as a help to the garden or to scrub down the concrete outside the back of the house. There were no drains anywhere in the village for wastewater disposal. It was all left to the forces of nature and gravity.

The main living room was at the rear of the house, and had been built on as an extension before we moved in. This was the room where we spent virtually all of our time. It was always warm, and there were chairs for everybody along one side and at the ends of the table, with an extra large chair on either side of the fireplace. In addition to the chairs a long backless form ran along one side of the table, against the wall......for boys.

The table was a very versatile piece of furniture. For general use it had a normal top, that was scrubbed almost every day, but when the place had to be tidy for visitors, the tabletop could be turned over, to reveal a highly polished top. Mansion Polish (with a picture of two mice skating on a highly polished surface) on the tin lid was applied almost every day, and woe-betide any boy that came along with sticky fingers. Mother had a long handled hairbrush that seemed to be used for the wrong purpose sometimes, and was always handy. Apart from its normal use, the table has on occasions been transferred to the "front room" and used as an operating table for minor surgery. I had my back teeth extracted under anaesthetic on this table and Ray had his tonsils removed on it.

At the end of the table father had his large upright wooden armchair, where he would sit and read his Farmer And Stockbreeder, (the new name for the Farm, Field and Fireside) after his day's work was done. When father was in this chair, and he said, "Hush......... Less noise", that is exactly what he meant.

A black iron cooking stove and oven that had to be relit every morning kept the whole house warm. That stove was what most housewives were very proud of, although secretly I think that they must have hated the things. Two or three times a week the Zebo or some other sort of black lead polish would come out, with a curved brush to apply the polish, another of the same shape to polish with, and then a cloth to add the final polish. The final result would be a gleaming black stove, and a housewife with black arms and often a smudged face where an arm had been used to wipe off the sweat.

A black fender was kept around the front and sides of the stove to act as a warning, not to get too close. In a box inside the fender where it was nice and warm, especially when the weather turned chilly, Nell, our little terrier dog had her special spot.

There was always a kettle of hot water sitting immediately over the fire, with the round removable disc top of the stove underneath the kettle removed to keep it on the boil. In those days we used to listen to the kettle "singing". I don't know if it was the iron that the kettle was made of or the gentle heat of the fire, or it could have been a combination of the two, but the kettles gave out a gentle semi whistling noise before coming to the boil. Beside it would be another kettle "getting warm" to be used next.

We didn't take a lot of notice in those days, but the steam escaping from those kettles must have contributed to all the wonderful patterns that appeared on the inside of all the window panes on frosty winter mornings.

On the wooden moulded uprights that were giving the impression of holding up the mantle shelf, over the fireplace, the brass studded fire bellows hung on one side. On the other side hung the toaster. Not the bright chrome electrical device that we use today, but a fork with three prongs. Made of wire it had a sliding extension to the handle, and the dread was dangled in front of, or over the ember coals of the fire. There were occasions.....no, let us tell the truth..... many occasions, when the fire had not been lit very long in the mornings, that there was a choice of smoky bread from unburned coal or wood, or the bread fall off the thin prongs and become a burnt offering, that may or may not be retrieved. We were not all that keen on toast in the mornings. On the shelf above the stove were two blue decorated glass bowls, where all sorts of little bits were deposited, to be retrieved later.

On a wet day it was a treat to get those treasure boxes down and see what could be found. The glass bowls shared the mantle with two golden coloured tall glass vases and an old fashioned alarm clock with a bell at the top that would be hit by the little mechanical hammer at the appointed hour at what seemed to be the middle of the night.

There was lino on the floor and a few rugs scattered around, which made it a bit warmer underfoot. A large window at the garden end was not always to the advantage of small boys. Whenever you were doing something that was not strictly approved of, there was always somebody looking out of that window to wag a disapproving finger... or maybe worst. The room was no palace, but we lived in it quite comfortably and happily.

The garden at the rear was used as a play area, where Ray and I made our trolleys with sets of wheels that had once been fitted to someone's pram. At the far end of the garden was the earth closet, in a draughty barn like building. I could never understand why the doors of these places always seem to have that saw edge zigzag at the tops of the doors. It couldn't have been for extra air or ventilation, there was already at least a foot gap at the top, and another foot gap at the bottom. And six bricks removed to form a pattern in the rear end wall.

Next door was the "Linhay" where everything was kept. Coal, firewood, gardening tools, bikes and Uncle Art's old B.S.A motor bike. It had been there for years, a monster of a thing, with a long petrol tank, and high cow-horn type handlebars. Ray and I spent a lot of time when it was wet trying to get it started, but we never managed it. All we got was a severe kick back on occasions when we put all our weight on the kick-start. The floor was rough cobbles and very uncomfortable to play games on, so the serious games like marbles were played indoors or out in the road.

On the far side of this treasure-trove was the "wash house" where the copper boiler was installed with its cast iron smoke stack. Part of the boy's job when we were old enough was to make sure that there was enough dry kindling wood and long logs to keep the boiler going for an hour or two to boil the washing.

Early in the morning mother would go off to the steaming "copper" armed with large blocks of Puritan or Hudson's Soap and packets of Rinso or Soako, to wage war on the dirty washing. Water had to be carried to the washhouse and the boiler filled, while extra buckets stood around to fill the zinc bath, taken down from its nail on the wall and used for rinsing the clothes.

All the time that the clothes were boiling away in the copper, mother would lift the lid and give the contents a few prods and a turn with her "copper stick", a stubby piece of wood about three feet long, kept especially for the purpose.

Washing was hung out to dry on a line stretched the whole length of the garden. In the centre was a prop, to hold the washing clear of the ground, and to give a little extra height and catch any extra wind to speed up the drying. That prop was a long straight pole with a fork at one end that supported the line. How many times that prop was found broken or half broken I cannot remember, but those boys were always in trouble for damaging it. When the washing was dried (or maybe not, when the weather was wet), all the washing was collected in a flasket, a large oval shaped basket. That evening the table was mother's to do the ironing on.

Flat irons replaced the kettles on the top of the fire to get hot. When considered hot enough the iron would be slipped into a tin shoe that was polished on the base, and held in place by a pair of spring levers. How did you know when the iron was hot enough? There was no thermostats or other means to tell you, so the answer was easy. You just spat on it, and if it flew off, then it was hot enough. Shirts, jackets, dresses and everything else was given the ironing treatment. The occasional scorch mark because the iron was too hot was not completely unknown.

At night the paraffin lamps would be lit, and the candles prepared in the candlestick holder in readiness for bedtime, or as a small light in the scullery. If the boys were going to be allowed to read in bed, we would be able to take a small hand lamp to the bedroom, otherwise it would probably be a candle that had to be put out as quickly as possible. Paraffin lamps were not the best things to see to read or draw with, so games were often used to pass away the evenings.

Meccano was too much trouble to be taken out evenings, and if screws were dropped there was no way that you could find them again in the poor light. This bit of engineering was left until there were days off or holidays.

We could read a little but the light was not really suitable, so we had to make sure that the adventures of Teddy Tail in the Daily Mail and the cartoon strip Mr. Ruggles was read in daylight if possible. Mother was usually occupied during the evenings with knitting of socks. She used to have four steel knitting needles that would click away for hours at a time. She didn't seem to need any light, she knew exactly what to do, and over the years must have knitted hundreds of socks.

During the daytime if she had any time to spare, out would come the Jones hand operated sewing machine. She was always making clothes for someone in the family.

Boys were expected to enter this part of domestic life too. Wool was bought in skeins, just as it had been taken off the looms. Boys were made to sit with arms outstretched with the wool over each hand, while mother wound the wool into a ball. It used to make your arms ache like mad, especially if someone happened to call at the door and delay the winding.

Bedtimes were usually fairly early, we all had to be up early in the mornings, father to do the milking before he went to work, at Holwood, and children to walk to school before nine o'clock. There was usually an odd job or two to do before setting out on that long walk to Tideford. Everybody was expected to do their share of the work.

Ray and I were usually responsible for getting the day's water supply. We had to carry the bucket to the old village pump that served the lower half of the village, and pump it full of water. By holding the handle of the bucket low down on either side we were expected to carry it home. Easier said than done. Firstly, very often the pump had to be primed, it was very old and the seal that held a drop of water to seal the mechanism didn't hold water very well, and the pump had to be primed from above.

To prime meant pouring water in the top of the pump, so it wasn't a lot of good going to fetch water with no reserve of water to start with. As the mechanics of the pump had a wooden casing around it to prevent freezing up in winter, it added to the problems of very small boys trying to pour water in the top off the wooden casing, but when it came to pouring in water you had to estimate where the centre of the mechanism was to pour water in. Sometimes it turned out to be a very wet task, and the whole operation was a bit like the song, "There's a hole in your bucket," in reverse.

The question of the pump handle came next. To get a good flow of water the pump needed a good long stroke, a thing that was almost impossible when you are not tall enough to lift the lever to the top. To avoid getting wet feet with any surplus water that came out after pumping had stopped, a granite trough was placed under the spout, with a hole drilled at one end to allow surplus water to run out and down the roadside gutter. Fine for grown ups, but when the water hit the top edge of the trough, small boys got knees and socks wet.

To carry a bucket of water between two people is fine if you are the same size and can keep in step. We weren't, and to get through that passageway that wasn't quite wide enough usually resulted in wet stockings and feet and not a few fights.

Our main garden was at the extreme end of the village, on the Saltash side of the Chapel where all the vegetables were grown. Carrots, turnips, cabbages and potatoes all stood in straight lines like soldiers. Nothing was allowed out of place. Everything had to be correct in father's garden. There was no place for errors. He was proud of the garden and the quality of the vegetables that he grew.

CHAPTER 6 - OUTSIDE WORK

Down in the lower far corner, all the waste from the garden that could not be fed to the pigs was piled against the hedge and held in place by some wire netting. Today it would be referred to as a compost heap, but to us it was just the rubbish pile, that would soon rot down to be put back on the garden. Beside it would be a couple of buckets that had outlived their usefulness and the bottoms had been removed. With an insulation of straw on the inside, they were now brought into use to force a few early sticks of rhubarb. The main crop would have huge umbrellas, and packed so closely together that the ground underneath would be kept very dry, requiring the odd bucket of water to help the crop along. The stalks of rhubarb were always up to the standard of father's crops, huge in diameter and length. And what good tarts it made.

No room here for "that bloody new fangled artificial manure stuff, you can't use anything better than good old fashioned cow sh** (dung)". I suppose we were as near to being self-supporting as it was possible to get. We kept up to three cows to keep us in milk, cream and butter. There were always a few pigs in the field to either go to market when ready, or with the occasional pig being shared by someone else, to fill a trundle with pork and bacon for our own use.

The trundle was like half a wooden barrel with a loose lid. When pigs were killed the carcase was jointed and packed away in salt in the trundle, and joints removed as needed. It was usual to share with a neighbour so that the meat got used up in a reasonable time. That way there was less risk of it going bad or getting too salty to eat. Next time around, the neighbour would supply the pig. The trundle was the equivalent of today's deep freeze, but not so efficient, or convenient.

A hundred or so hens kept us supplied with eggs. Any surplus was sent to Market with the cream and butter. All the stock was kept in the field across the road. The cows were driven to the "top field" and brought back each day for milking for part of the year. That field was normally kept mainly for grass to turn into hay and winter fodder. Behind the shippon were a couple of pig and hen houses. A small Dutch barn type building provided cover for wood and hayricks.

All farm workers were given the opportunity to have a hedge of wood in those days. Not any old hedge. The lease on farms dictated how many years a hedge had had to be allowed to grow before cutting down and be re-laid, usually six or seven years. It really meant that all the wood on their hedge was theirs for the taking, but............ it had to be cut and removed in their own time and the hedge repaired and the remaining wood "laid" properly to ensure a cattle proof hedge and wood supplies in year to come. And the farmer had it all done for him.......FREE.

Thin twiggy wood was cut in about three foot lengths and bound together by flexible sticks to form three faggots. All the other wood, up to about 6 inches in diameter, were cut into logs using a handsaw, with the wood held on a "sawing horse". Larger diameter lengths of wood were cut into logs using a cross cut saw, with a friendly neighbour working one end of the saw, while father worked the other end. The logs were then split into convenient sizes by a sharp axe.

As the faggots had to be thoroughly dried for use as kindling wooed, it was put to work whilst drying out. Faggots were used to form a base for hayricks. They would keep the precious hay off the ground, let any water pass underneath, and let the faggots dry out at the same time.

After use the faggots would be transferred to their own square rick, and used for firewood, or used again as a base for hayricks. Nothing was wasted, or only used once when it could be used twice.

The faggot wood had to be broken or cut into short lengths, by the boys of the house. The small brittle ends and very dry sticks presented no problems, but the thicker sticks had to be cut with a patch hook, using a log as an anvil. Old country folks reckoned that before a new patch hook was ever used, the handle should be removed, and the metal portion of the hook should be placed on top of a hedge, in the open, to "allow two moons to pass over it" to prevent the hook becoming rusty, and to keep a keen cutting edge. I think that something must have gone wrong with the hooks we were allowed to use, the edge was never very keen.

Milking was carried out twice a day, early mornings and late afternoon. The cows were tied up and fed in the shippon, and the little three legged stool and shiny zinc bucket would be placed in position. Father would turn the peak of his cap to the rear, lean his head against the side of the cow, and milking would be done by hand while the cows were feeding and contented. Tails would sometimes swish and hit the milker's face and a few words would be said about the stupid animal. Occasionally a cow would kick out and milker, bucket and stool would either be deposited in an undignified position on the floor, or maybe almost outside the door. Then real strong words would be used.

After milking, the milk that was going to be made into cream would be taken in pails to the scullery and transferred to large enamel pans, and allowed to stand for what seemed an awful long time to allow the cream to come to the top. There was always a double burner oil stove burnings, and the pans would be placed on the oil stoves and allowed to gently heat the milk to allow the cream to form on the top. An asbestos mat was placed between stove and pan to avoid a hot spot developing, and the milk "burning". When the cream had formed and the milk had cooled, the cream was skimmed off the top with a "skimmer", a kind of metal plate with holes drilled all over, and a small handle fitted to the side. The skimmer would be slipped under the cream and any milk collected would run out of the holes. The lovely thick crusty cream was put into glass dishes to cool, and become even thicker, ready to send off to Market, or made into butter. I must admit that we did eat a fair share, with jam, fruit pies or anything else. Apple tart and cream are irresistible.

Surplus cream was made into butter by my mother between the hundreds of other jobs that she seemed to do. The cream would be turned over in its bowl hundreds of times by hand, until it started to become thicker. A little salt would be added while the cream was being gently folded into itself, and after what seemed an eternity the golden butter would appear.

The butter scales would be brought out, a spotless pair of scales with brass weights, and a circular white marble slab in the place where the container would normally be fitted to household scales. A lump of butter would be placed on the marble and the weight adjusted until it was exactly half a pound. When the weight was correct the butter would be roughly rounded up and placed on a "pat" for finishing. The "pat" was like a wooden mushroom upside down, with the stem for a handle. The flat top had a carved surface, usually a sheaf of corn or something similar. The butter would be placed on top and shaped, like a Christmas pudding. The butter would be taken off the "pat" and all the half-pound pats of butter would sit on square pieces of greaseproof paper and placed on a marble slab, ready for market.

Mr. Ough from Quethiock would call around about twice a week to collect butter, cream and eggs in his dark green Morris Cowley van, and take them to market in Plymouth. Surplus milk was mixed with the food given to the pigs, or fed to the young calves, when they were fed by hand, immediately after weaning. Another job for the boys. The calves were offered two fingers to suck, as a substitute for their mother's teat. Whilst sucking the fingers, you hand was lowered into a bucket of milk, and the young calf would drink a full meal.

During the winter months both morning and evening milking was carried out in the shippon by the light of the hurricane lantern, hung from a convenient wall. By today's standards it would be considered very dangerous, with the amount of dry straw that was around.

Straw for bedding for all the animals was stored under the Dutch barn building, and in the corn store at the end of the shippon. This was one thing that had to be bought in, either for cash or with labour, usually the latter.

All the smallholders and farmers had an agreement, which was usual in those days. They all depended on each other to help with the work at times. There were no records kept, people knew how much labour was owed to each other, and there was never a word said because someone hadn't done their share. No one asked for help. When needed the neighbour's would just arrive and get on with the harvesting or whatever was needed. Items like straw were exchanged the same way.

It was not unusual that if a disaster hit a farm or homestead the loss would be made good by the surrounding neighbours. No one would need to ask for help, it would be readily available. There was no such thing as house or house contents insurance in those days. Even if there was, it would be too expensive for the farm workers.

The farm animals were the main assets of all the small holders and they got priority in all things. My father's animals wanted for nothing. They were always well fed, warm and dry. He loved all animals and would never allow an animal to be ill treated. When he sat down at night there was always two or three cats waiting to climb up on him and spend the evening purring away on his lap.

Horses were his real love. We didn't keep a horse but he worked with horses all day at Holwood Farm. He was a Driver in the Royal Artillery during the war, and would only talk about the horses that he had handled in Flanders or on the Khyber Pass if we asked him about the war.

His horses were his world. When he walked into a field, even on a strange farm, horses seemed to sense that he was almost one of them and would come right over to him without being called. He would never ask a horse to do anything that was not within their capabilities, or liable to cause them injury. After the war he had driven horses between Holwood Farm and St Germains Quay to collect lime in wagons to spread on the land. There were occasional accidents on Heskyn Hill, and horses got injured. Other drivers only used one drag shoe under the rear wheels to slow the loaded wagon down, but I have heard them say that Father always used two, even if it was much slower. He went to the extremes, I have been told, of placing damp cloths over the nostrils of his horses when the weather was dry, and the lime was very dusty.

CHAPTER 7 - OUR DEFICIENCIES

As you must have assumed by now, the village was completely devoid of any Public Utilities. Electricity was only a dream. When we, as small children saw it first, it was like some sort of magic. I can always remember, going to a house in Callington and watching in amazement as the lights went on at the press of a switch. Electricity didn't come to the village until after the war (1956). The carpenter shop would have benefitted from electricity to power the band saw used to cut wheel rims for carts, which seemed to be the most regular job. As things stood they had to start a stationary engine to drive any power tools, via a selection of pulleys and belts.

There were no such things then as washing machines or spin driers, and such things as toasters were not generally available even if you had electricity. I think most people would have been contented with just a good light to read or sew with.

Television had not been invented.

We had no mains water supply in the area, so all drinking water came from wells, and came to the houses by hand pump or a bucket on the end of a rope pulled up by windlass. Holwood farmhouse was the only house in the area that had running water and a bathroom. All of that water had to be pumped to a tank in the roof from a wall every morning. With all the talk of lead poisoning we hear these days we should not have survived. All the water we ever drank came out of a pump with a lead spout and often lead pipes.

The nearest telephone was at Penpol Farm, one of the old Manor Houses, in the area and being farmed by Mr. Cannon. That was half a mile away from the village by road, but there was a path across the fields that cut the distance considerably. Mrs. Cannon or her daughter wouldn't use the phone if it could be avoided. Only the people who actually owned a phone would know how to use such a modern invention anyway, so it was not the usual request to use someone's phone. We tried not to have emergencies that required the use of a phone.

We did have a fire one Sunday morning, in the kitchen of Alf and Bessie Jane, our next-door neighbours. Vic Wythe went to Penpol to telephone for the fire brigade, but the fire was put out with buckets of water, hurriedly pumped from the wells at both ends of the village. Later that afternoon a Fire Officer on a motorcycle arrived to see if assistance was still needed. The fire call had been put through to Callington as being the nearest town with a fire engine. Unfortunately they couldn't arrange for another set of horses to change on the way so couldn't come to the fire. The town of Callington only had a horse drawn fire engine until the end of 1931, and then only if the horses were not already out working, drawing the carrier's wagon.

The nearest Petrol pumps to our village were at Tideford, so people who ran small market lorries, or farmers who ran cars had to keep cans of petrol handy or make sure that there was plenty in the tank.

We didn't boast the luxury of a shop. Anything that was needed was either delivered by various tradesmen or collected by a walk to one of the larger villages, or the alternative was hoping the boys would collect it when they went to school at Tideford.

Father's tobacco was a different story. He needed that a couple of times a week. Then I had to walk to Pounda, on St Ive road to get Digger Plug from Mrs. Pooley, after the Hoopers left the district. Mr. and Mrs. Pooley with their daughter Isobell lived in a very neatly painted house next door to the blacksmith's shop at Pounda, where Mr. Pooley had been the village blacksmith for many years.

That little square block of Digger Plug tobacco, with the picture of a bearded head of a sailor on the yellow packet, which was then the trademark of John Players Tobacco Company, cost 4d an ounce (about 1 ? p). The little package had to be safely hidden away in a pocket to make sure Mr. Berryman, the local bobby, didn't see it. There were laws about children buying tobacco in those days.

We had no lighting other than candles or paraffin lamps. These had to have the wicks trimmed every few days, as they burnt down and became hard and uneven, giving an uneven flame and nasty smell. The very thin and fragile glass globe would get a smoky film on the inside, so needed cleaning almost every day. I was very fond of drawing and painting, but paraffin lighting was not the best light for the pastime. Two lights in a room might have made a difference, but harsh economics dictated that there would only be one.

Paraffin for lighting came with either the coal man, Mr. Tabb from Tideford, or Mr. Eugene Harris from Quethiock, the grocer, who arrived with his 30 cwt Morris Commercial lorry on Monday mornings. He carried a large container of paraffin at the front of the lorry, groceries at the rear.

We stored our paraffin as everybody else seemed to, in two Pratts petrol cans. These were very useful cans. Oblong in shape with a brass screw cap, which made it easy to pour the contents into an old enamel jug with a spout to transfer the oil to the lamps. The biggest problem seemed to be how to get rid of the smell from clothes when some of the paraffin got wasted, as it very often did, no matter how careful you were.

There was no such thing as refuse collection until 1935, when we were informed that there would be a collection of household refuse on every fourth Friday. That caused trouble. We all had to have a dustbin, but we had no shops. Mr. Wythe went to Saltash on the bus to get his, but he wasn't allowed to bring it home on the bus after he had bought it. Eventually Alf Jane came to the rescue with his lorry. He made a special trip to Saltash and bought a bulk order, for almost everyone in the village.

Until now, kitchen waste went to the pigs. Cinders and ashes were always in demand for garden paths and metal objects were thrown in a communal tip between the bank opposite the Chapel and the hedge behind it. This would soon rust away. Glass would break into millions of pieces, and anything else would be checked over by any enterprising boy that happened to come along.

Obviously, the Council had not given a lot of thought to the thing. Where were boys going to get spares to keep their trolleys and boneshaker bikes on the road now? All the good things were going to end up in the back of that little Karrier truck with the curved sliding doors over the rear body.

CHAPTER 8 - LONDON CALLING

As there was not a lot to do in the evenings and those boys were getting older, the possibilities of a wireless set was investigated. Some coloured leaflets arrived one day from a firm called Andrewatha from Plymouth, who were having a sales drive in the area. Father thought long and hard and then decided that he didn't want to deal with a firm in Plymouth. They were probably "cheap jacks anyway". It was decided that we would have one as soon as possible, but things had to be considered very carefully before rushing into buying such a luxury.

A suitable place to put the thing had to be considered, and if a shelf was needed to keep it out of the reach of boys, what size shelf and where?

A lot of leaflets arrived and eventually a Cossar Superhette was ordered from Mr. Harris of Criffle Mill, near Cutmere, who was the local electrical genius. He had electric lights everywhere, all generated from the huge water wheel at the side of the mill. He had a room full of glass storage batteries that gave him light and power when the water wheel was not turning.

The size of the wireless was discussed with Bill Jane, and he made a suitable shelf. Eventually the shelf was fitted to the wall above where father always sat at the end of the table in the living room.

Two very long poles were found and put up in the garden, one each end, with a length of wire between them, and a hole drilled through the window frame for one end of the wire to join the wireless.

Eventually the day arrived when the wonder set arrived with Mr. Harris delivering it with his motorbike and sidecar. It was taken out of the box and the huge 120-volt battery was fitted, plus the acid filled glass accumulator, and the great turn on took place.

I can remember it was on a Saturday and the first thing that we heard was a news bulletin. There was a demonstration of the other wavelengths available on such an up to date set, but it was turned back to the National Programme where they had sensible programmes.

Being only a small boy, with not much knowledge about the world outside the village I was amazed for quite a long time how easy it was to stop all the traffic in a large town. It could be done, I knew, because every Saturday night the announcer would say, "Stop. Once again we stop the roar of London's traffic to bring you some of the interesting people who are IN TOWN TONIGHT", and you could hear all the noise of the traffic stop. An hour later he would say, "Carry on London", and all the cars would start up again. We were always allowed to listen to Monday Night at Seven. But had to miss a lot of it when it became Monday Night at Eight.

As small boys that had not yet been taught about time changes in other parts of the world, there was a very confusing programme on Saturday evenings called Five Hours Back, all about what was going on in America. It all got sorted out after a while. I was not the only one to be confused over what was said over the wireless.

Before every News broadcast there would be S.O.S Messages for people urgently needed due to illness or accident in their family. I can remember Ray wondering why everybody who sent out an S.O.S had "Lost their dog" (last heard of).

We didn't get to hear Children's Hour very often, as we were still on the way home from school when it started. I did complain to the BBC by letter about this once, but didn't get a reply. Perhaps the letter is still waiting to be answered.

The accumulators would run down after about two weeks if the wireless wasn't used too much. When it ran down the sound would gradually get quieter until it just couldn't be heard. Then we had to walk to Cutmere to get a recharged accumulator. There was an arrangement that they would be delivered, but they always ran out at the wrong time.

There were times when the cost of a recharged accumulator was not readily available too. Sixpence (2 1/2 p) was a lot to have spare in those days when every penny was earmarked. That accumulator was heavy to carry both ways, the discharged one having to be taken on the outward trip. Then there was the added hazard of spilling acid. When it came around time to fit a new 120-volt battery, father usually did the carrying on his bike. They measured about four inches deep, and fourteen inches square and were very heavy. These lasted about three months and in 1931 cost eleven shillings, about one third of a week's wages for farm workers.

We children were not supposed to touch such a piece of high technology. Father was the official 'turner on' for a long time. However, eventually we were able to turn it on and off, but no more. Most embarrassing though when it had been turned off in a hurry after turning on without getting permission, and no time to get it back on the right station. It's moments like this that get young boys found out.

Before this piece of advanced technology was introduced to the house, we were not exactly without entertainment. Our in-house music was supplied by a H.M.V. wind up type gramophone, with a huge horn, on which we played our collection of 78 r.p.m. records. Often the main spring would fail to stand the pressure of boys winding it up tight, and there would be a loud springing sound, the winding handle would fly around, and there would be no music until father repaired it once more. The trouble was that every time it was repaired at home the spring was shortened an inch or two as no replacements were to hand. This meant that there was not enough spring remaining to play a full side of the record.

The H.M.V label showed a dog listening to a gramophone like ours, with his head tilted to one side. We tried to get Nell to listen like that, but "Horsey Keep Your Tail Up" didn't appeal to her. Perhaps we should have tried harder with "Horsey, Horsey, don't you stop, just let your feet go clipety clop".

I think that one of the major problems was keeping the needles in the correct boxes. We used to have little needles that had to be fitted to the sound box every two or three records, to give a reasonable sound, and to keep the sound box in the correct groove. Needles were sixpence for a box of "Songster" needles, but the worn needles would either get put back in the box with the new needles, or the whole lot would get upset.......... Then there was real trouble.

CHAPTER 9 – THE CARPENTER AND THE BLACKSMITH

For most of the old villages the carpenter and the blacksmith shops were the most important places in the village. The locals relied on them for everything, from making a crib for the newborn baby to making the coffin for the last journey. The blacksmith made or repaired all things metal, from the leaking kettle to a broken plough.

It was said that the village of Blunts once kept three blacksmiths in full employment. To make up this number the blacksmith shop at Pounda must have been included, as well as the blacksmith which at one time was the building which we used as a corn store, in addition to the blacksmith's shop next to the Church.

The original carpenter shop for the village was the one, that in my days, was operated by Mr. Bates and his son at Pounda, until the new one was built for the Janes by Squire Coryton next to the blacksmith. When I lived in the village both the carpenter shop and blacksmith shop at Blunts were operated by one man (Bill Jane) with help from friends.

Mr. Buller operated the blacksmith shop at Pounda as a one-man business. As a small boy I spent a lot of time in the blacksmith shop at Blunts, watching Bill Jane making up steel tyres for cart or wagon wheels. After making and putting together new sections of the wheel rims, (fellies) the wheel would be taken to the blacksmith shop where it would be laid on the large circular steel plate that lay on the ground outside the door. I seem to remember that for smaller wheels there was a smaller granite slab with a central hole set into the ground nearby.

With the aid of a measuring wheel, the outside circumference of the wooden wheel would be accurately measured, making allowances for joints that were not fully closed. The inside of the iron tyre would be made with the same internal diameter. The wheel tyre would be treated to a cherry red all round.

Not an easy task. When fully heated the tyre would be placed over the wheel by four men, holding the rim with long tongs. The blacksmith would hit the tyre into place and it would be shrunk into place by gently pouring water over it. On occasions it didn't work first time, but there were not many mistakes.

There always seemed to be a lot of small jobs waiting to be done, but nobody seemed in a hurry. During the grass-cutting season and again during corn cutting, farmers were in a hurry to get broken knives repaired, and occasionally they were lucky.

Although Bill Jane didn't do very much in the way of making implements, other blacksmiths in the area would make hay rakes and other farm machinery. The blacksmith at St Mellion had made the massive eight horse ploughs that were used to plough the land on Wiverton Down, to convert it to good farmland from its moorland state, in the late 1880s. It is interesting to note that the wooden patterns for the forgings used in the manufacture of these ploughs were made at the Blunts carpenter shop, by Bill Jane's father.

The blacksmith shop, which dated from the early 16th Century, had a stable type door. Although the doors were closed at night, it was only a gesture. There was no way that it could act as a security measure, as would be required today.

Earth floors were common in those days, but it was difficult to see that the floor was earth. It lay under a thick film of a mixture of coal dust and debris that had accumulated over many years. The walls were thick with the smoke and soot that had been generated by centuries of use by the open forge in the centre of the building.

Everywhere you looked, there were bits of iron either lying on the floor or leaning against the blackened walls. Dozens of tongs and other odd looking tools, mostly home made, were hung on walls or leaning against the huge block of wood that acted as a base for the anvil. Every tool seemed to be for a specific purpose, and Bill Jane knew exactly where the correct tool was, despite the confusion. As new jobs came into the workshop, they were found a convenient place to lie, until someone remembered the item. There was no system of recording or booking in jobs as we would today. However, everybody seemed satisfied, and jobs did get done.

The blacksmith shop at Pounda was operated by Mr. Buller, who was also the local farrier. There were always horses tied up outside waiting for new shoes to be fitted. The fire would be stirred into life by the huge hand bellows beside the forge and a few deft movements with the little shovel , and rattled around with the poker until it burst into life, throwing up a fierce flame from the centre, like a miniature volcano. Horseshoes would be put in the fire and heated until bright red, then removed, and a new one tried for size. It would probably take two or three fittings before the smith was fully satisfied with the fit. Only then would the iron shoe be thrown on the floor to cool and normalise, before being fitted to the horse with special nails.

The shop itself was a really dirty place. Everything you touched was covered with a thick coating of black dust. When a big job was being heated and forged it was a wonderful sight. The fire would roar as air from the bellows was pumped into it causing a multicoloured fountain of sparks to leap from the centre. When the iron was removed and taken to the anvil, sparks would fly in all directions as the hammers forged the metal into the shape required. After every couple of strikes to the metal, the hammer would be given a bouncing motion on the anvil. That sound seemed to ring all over the district. Although it wasn't noticeable at the time, when boys got home a sharp eyed mother would always notice the little holes burnt into clothes by the red hot sparks.

Just like the blacksmith shop at Blunts, the whole place was littered with tools of various shapes and sizes, most of which had probably not been used since they were made for some special purpose in the long forgotten past. With blackened cobwebs shrouding the tools they resembled instruments of torture from another era.

This was a very busy shop, with a continuous stream of tools and implements to be repaired. Most of the time they were required urgently. Farmers never waste money, having tools repaired, until they are sure that they will be used.

Mr. Buller was a very tall gent, well over six feet tall, and made a striking figure riding his huge cycle to and from to Landrake where he lived. The cycle itself was of the type that was made especially for oversize policemen.

Two top crossbars were fitted with an extra strengthening bar extending from the top of the headset to the bottom bracket. He was a familiar figure, heading towards Landrake at all times of the nights, with his huge bag of tools on his handlebars. They were an essential part of his equipment, to carry out small repairs on the way home. To earn a bit of "baccy" money is how he described those jobs.

Every night on the way home he would stop in the village on some pretext and scrounge a cup of tea from someone. He was always filthy dirty with black dust and soot. He always seemed to be wearing the same jacket. It wasn't just dirty, it shone with the dirt, and cracks would appear in the thick dirt on the sleeves. He looked the same on his way to work in the mornings too.

During the winter months it seemed to be taken for granted that Dickie Buller would call in to someone's house to borrow a bit of Carbide to fill his cycle lamp.

There was a sharp contrast between the two carpenters shops. Mr. Bates at Pounda always had a neat and tidy shop, both inside and outside.

There were very few shavings on the floor left from one day to the next and it would appear that there was a system where all tools were put into their allotted place at the end of the day. Outside there were no old wagons or wheels waiting to be repaired, that had waited so long that they were just a heap of useless junk. The carpenter shop itself had a neat and tidy look about it, window frames were painted and doors were well hung and painted. Even windows were clean enough to let daylight in.

Bill Jane's carpenter shop was, shall we say, different, with unpainted and poorly hung doors and a patched up wood and galvanise front to the building. The earth floor had remained unseen for many years, and was covered in shavings and sawdust, plus a generous supply of small bits of wood. Inside there were two long workbenches that had to be cleared of tools and miscellaneous debris as each new job was allocated a space for repair. There never appeared to be a special home for any tool, but it was difficult to see if Bill Jane was looking for something that he could not find. He was such a calm sort of fellow, very soft spoken and slow moving and he never appeared to be in a hurry. Folk in the village always said that he was a very good tradesman, even if he was a little slow to do the jobs, but he did make up for it when it came to writing out the bills.

Inside the shop was a very large pedestal drill and a large band saw, both driven by a series of belts and pulleys from the stationary engine housed in a lean to outside. This was a very old engine, a Perkins I seem to remember, that could on occasions be a little temperamental to start. Threats would be made to get rid of it, but I am given to understand that it was still in use until the carpenter shop was demolished in 1987.

When on occasions the band saw blade would break it was removed and repaired by brazing with a huge brazing lamp, like an oversize blowlamp. How that place didn't burst into flames many times over the years I will never know.

There was always a pleasant smell of a mixture of new wood, linseed oil and paint around the place, with an oil stove to heat the essential kettle for tea in the corner. Outside in the area in front of the shop stood a collection of old wagons and other debris that at some stage in the distant past had been brought with the hope of a repair being carried out. Somewhere along the line, it had been overlooked or forgotten, and it is doubtful if the owners would ever remember or even recognise their property.

The previously mentioned stationary engine was the motive power behind the large saw bench that stood in the yard, and was used to cut large planks of wood and the tree trunks that lay around the yard, waiting to be cut into convenient lengths as firewood.

CHAPTER 10 – THE ARM OF THE LAW

On the whole the boys around at that time didn't get up to too much mischief, the odd window did get broken or some minor misdemeanour. Helping ourselves to someone's apples was considered a legitimate crime, knowing full well that the worst that could happen was a clip around the ear, and not even that if you could run fast enough.

But we were all terrified of Mr. Berryman, and would hide away if he came to the village. He was one of the old type coppers who believed that a clip around the ear did more good than anything else, and there was less paperwork. Not many crimes were committed that needed his attention, he usually came in to inspect records of cattle and pig movements to market etc., or to remind people of new regulations as they came out.

One such regulation that demanded a visit to almost every house in the Landrake area was what we knew as the "tailwaggers" regulation. About 1931 all cycles had to have a white patch, six inches long, to be fitted to the rear mudguard. This patch of white became known as a "tailwagger", why, I shall never know. This was an occasion when every house had to be visited and informed. Once you had been told, there could be no excuse if you were caught breaking the law afterwards.

He was a huge man, with a bright red face. You could almost imagine him singing "The Laughing Policeman". Yes, that song was around in those days.

What the boys could never work out was how he always seemed to know what you had been up to, and if you were letting your halo slip a little, why was Mr. Berryman the only person who came along at exactly the wrong moment.

Then he seemed to have great delight in telling parents what you had been doing. That meant more questions, and then more little adventures would come out, not always to our advantage.

Until about 1934 there had always been a wooden three-armed direction post at the junction of Broad Road and the Callington to Tideford road. This post had always been high up on the hedge of a

Holwood field, and always seemed to be at an angle. The County Council decided to replace this with a new metal sign mounted on a tubular pillar, much lower down, and fitted in the centre of the little triangular plot of waste ground formed in the centre of the three roads. This was fine, and made a wonderful place to swing. It wasn't long before the post became loose, and the whole thing could easily be swing around. When you are young and you leave one game to move on to the next, it doesn't always enter your mind to see that everything is as it should be. Mr. Berryman visited every house where there were boys to point out that there were people around who didn't know the area, and ended up getting well and truly lost.

He did have a bit of a twinkle in his eye when he was telling us off though.

What position does that fingerboard occupy now? Back in the hedge where it started, although a little lower down, but still with a distinct lean towards the village.

CHAPTER 11 – VISITING TRADESMEN

Butcher Congdon came each week with his old Morris Light Van with a selection of meats on offer. He had a corner shop with windows that went right around the corner, on the main road at Tideford. Being the only butcher in the village, which was quite large, he seemed to do quite a brisk trade. The inside of the shop was painted white and all around the inside of the windows were hooks and rails from which were hung the half carcasses of lambs and pigs. Sides of beef were at the rear of the shop, where customers could admire and order their cuts of beef. When in season, rows of game would be strung up outside, all round the shop. At Christmas time turkeys and geese would take their place on the outside hooks. They wouldn't be taken in at night, the chances of anyone stealing them was very remote. A net was placed over the poultry, and the butcher or a night watchman would be sleeping nearby.

The butcher's son Bert drove the van around to all the villages on a different day of the week, to cater for the needs of customers in remote areas. The van was equipped with all the tools required – knives, choppers, saws and chopping block. The van was kept very clean with white painted interior where all the meat was hung on rails placed across the rear of the van. Down in one corner inside the rear door, a clean bit of muslin was placed every day to be used to wipe knives, chopping block and of course, hands that had to hold the steering wheel and handle money. Food poisoning was hardly ever heard of in those days but I suppose it must have happened.

Bread came to the village once a week from the bakery of the Menhenic family at Landrake. Theirs was a large Chevrolet one-ton van, painted navy blue with gold lettering. The rear was equipped with sliding trays to carry the bread. On special occasions, or when our powers of persuasion were strong enough, mother would get a nice brown loaf, with writing on the side, (Hovis) or our special treat, some "tuffs". When the rear doors of that van were opened there was a wonderful smell of freshly baked bread. Fancy cakes or anything other than plain normal loaves were something of a rarity. Such things were not the normal fare of a farming community in those days. Hot Cross buns at Easter were about the limit.

Our family didn't buy a great deal of bread. It was mostly home made. Saturday was normally baking day when bread and saffron cakes to last a week were baked, along with pasties for Ray and myself for dinners at school, and father at work. There was usually a second baking of pasties about Wednesday, so that they would be reasonably fresh.

On Friday evenings mother would mix up the dough for bread in a large white enamel pan and cover it in cloths and bring it into the living room. Another lot would be made up for the saffron cakes, and covered in the same way. When everybody had gone to bed the pans would be put on chairs in front of the warm stove and well covered. The warmth of the stove and the cloths would make the yeast work and the mixtures "rise".

Next morning the fire in the stove would get a few extra blows from the brass studded bellows, the damper would be fully opened in the flu above the stove, and the fire would soon start to roar and get the oven hot enough for baking. By the time the oven was hot enough the loaves of bread and cake would be lined up ready to take their place in the oven. What lovely smells came out of that kitchen and nothing tastes as good as hot bread and butter. Good thick butter that would melt on the hot bread, and run down the sides of your mouth. What better way to keep young boys happy.

Eugene Harris ran the general store at Quethiock, but left his wife to run it most days, so that he could visit all the outlying villages with is 30 cwt Morris Commercial lorry. The rear half of the truck would have groceries ordered by the various villagers the previous week. In case they had forgotten anything, or to cope with emergencies there were extra boxes of groceries and cleaning materials readily available in the back of the lorry.

Mr. Harris was a busy sort of gent with sharp ruddy features, and always in a hurry. He always wore a khaki coloured warehouse coat, unbuttoned and flying all ways. Over he shoulder he carried a leather money bag, and always seemed to make a big gesture of rattling the loose money as much as possible if he had to give change. Time was money he always said, and he tried to get in as much as he could of both every day.

Coal came from Tideford, delivered by Len Tabb. He only came about once a month, there was not a great deal of coal sold in the villages with plenty of free wood around. He was a small man who always seemed too small to lift a bag of coal off the back of a lorry, but he always seemed to manage. A thick sack turned with one corner inside the opposite corner made a kind of hood that he always put over his well-battered trilby when he had to carry coal. He is remembered mostly because he married my first schoolteacher.

The Insurance man, George Jeans from Callington came every few weeks to collect the life insurance money. Ray and myself had a Policy with Refuge Assurance that cost 1d a week. (That's two fifths of one new penny). Mr. Jeans came on an old motorbike with huge cow horn handlebars, a very long petrol tank and acetylene lighting. He always wore a long waterproof, oil-stained coat, and turned his cap front to rear when riding his motorbike, plus of course the obligatory goggles.

Household items came on the mobile bazaar that visited us on occasions. This was in the form of a lorry with a tent like structure on the back that doubled as living quarters for the two assistants. Outside, the rear was covered in hooks and rails, from which hung pots, pans, dishes, buckets and everything else that you care to mention. A tarpaulin covered the whole rear when it was travelling from one village to another. There was a certain amount of rattling from the load, but no one worried about that.

During the summer months we did get the Corona lorry call every two weeks with a selection of soft drinks. These were bought in cases of four bottles at a time. The selection was not always very good as our village was at the end of the day's round.

Those wire, clip down caps with a rubber seal did a very good job of keeping the bubbles in the drinks in the bottle. Of course there were odd times when they didn't seem to work so well, but it was usually when someone got disturbed having a crafty "swig" out of the bottle, and the top had to be replaced in a hurry, and didn't get closed properly.

The most welcome visitor during the summer was the Ice Cream van. Johno as he was always called, was a huge Italian who drove a wonderful green Morris Light Van. The rear upper panels of the van body had been replaced by sliding glass panels, through which he served the ice cream, from the containers below the steel covered bench. Johno used to shuffle himself from the drivers seat to squeeze between the benches to dip out a scoop of ice cream to place on that ½ d cone.

The van itself is worthy of a mention. Apart from being painted a bright green, there was a false flat roof over the whole bodywork, supported by a twisted brass pole at each corner. The false roof was edged by carved woodwork, with highlights picked out in gold paint. All over the body were gold painted scrolls and little painted countryside scenes. With gleaming brass radiator and axle hubs it was a very striking vehicle.

About 1934 someone from St Ive started a Fish and Chip round on one evening a week, with a coal burning fryer fitted into the back of a van. I can clearly remember this steaming shop on wheels, heralded by the very loud ringing of a hand bell, with in those days of almost complete silence during the hours of darkness, could be heard, long before it arrived. That was the moment when all the parents in the village would either go deaf, or find something that required their urgent attention. With hindsight, I think that it was an expensive delicacy, but we as children did win on occasions. There always seemed to be a lot of smoke and flames belching out of the smoke stack at the top. Mr. Algar did ask the driver on one occasion if he would mind parking on the other side of the road, away from the houses. As the fire settled down and the van drove away towards Landrake, there was a trail of sparks and smoke going off into the darkness.

As children, we thought that this was a great idea, as fish and chips were a luxury, very rarely seen in the country areas. However it didn't last very long. After a few weeks the visits came to a halt, and our taste of the exotic slipped away.

I suppose we must include the family doctor. Dr Jocelyn was a small, quiet spoken man with white hair, who came over from Callington in his Morris Cowley saloon car in time of need. He would prescribe pills and potions, but was usually able to supply most things from his bag. Minor surgery would be carried out by him, ably assisted by his partner, a gruff voiced Scott, Dr Aitken who didn't appear to be as popular. In 1935 Dr Jocelyn came with his flashy new car, an Austin Ten Saloon, reg. number J Y 3781. Very smart, all black and chrome, with a spare wheel on the back, covered with a metal cover that had a chrome strip around it. Very smart. There was no provision for a petrol can to be fitted to the running board, as was usual up to about this time.

CHAPTER 12 – NO PUB AND NO BEER

I have not yet mentioned a Public House. The parish of Quethiock was one of the very few parishes in the country that didn't have a Pub within its boundaries.

There was a pub in the village of Quethiock (The Masons Arms) until it closed in 1922 when the landlord died and left the premises to his son. The son decided to carry on as a farmer, and not to reopen the public house. Since that date, would-be drinkers there had to travel to The Butchers Arms in St Ive, The Commercial, (now the Rod and Line) at Tideford, or The Bullers Arms at Landrake.

All of these entailed a long walk or cycle ride home at the end of a hard day. That doesn't mean that the men of the village didn't enjoy a drink or two. Most houses had a shed or similar where a barrel of cider could be stored. A jug of cider was the usual thing on a lot of tables with the roast Sunday dinner. Not on ours, we were a strictly teetotal family. But we did have hot ginger wine at Christmas.

Between the cottages of Alf Jane and Granny Jane, were two little slate roofed sheds beside the road. They were originally built as pig stiles, large enough to raise two pigs in each. In the front, immediately beside the road there was a wall with stone sides where the pigs got their exercise, and where all the villagers fed the pigs on the household waste. The pigs became friends, but the friendship was short lived. Eventually the pigs had to be slaughtered, and as pigs were normally kept in two's one was divided among the villagers who had helped to feed them, and the other to the family.

Since the practice of everybody trying to keep a pig was discontinued, the pigs' houses have taken on another role. A good scrub out, a coat or two of lime wash and a wooden stand made by Bill Jane, and there was a prefect place to while away a Saturday afternoon, drinking cider that had found its way to that wooden stand. Many a happy afternoon was passed away in Alf Jane's pig house by half a dozen of his friends.

Many a good tale must have been told there, if the amount of laughter coming out of that little building, along with the large plumes of smoke, was anything to go by.

It was not the done thing to ask too many questions when you are small, but I did wonder at times why some of the men came out of those little sheds and had trouble getting to the end of the village, to get on the footpath across the field to Holwood.

At one time, many years before my time, Holwood Farm, like most other large farms and estates had a "cider house" where cider was made, stored and drunk by the workers. Something like a private public house with no restrictions. I knew where it was, near the farmhouse, but have no recollection of it being in use.

The rest of the village had a beer of sorts, all home made. Either Herb Beer that was made of a mixture of herbs, bough in packets from Mr. Harris, or a concoction made with genuine herbs. The hedges supplied sloes, damsons, and elder flowers that would be used with all sorts of fruits to make wines of varying degrees of potency. Elder wine was made in most houses, and Elderberries were made into "poor man's port".

Mango wurzles were normally grown as fodder for livestock, but "Wurzel Wine" was a lethal drink that only the hardened drinkers would drink......... if there was someone there to help them home.

This state of affairs had not always existed.

The large house mentioned earlier was until about 1865 the Star Inn. It seemed to have doubled as a lodging house at the same time. There seems to be no record when it opened its doors as an Ale House, but it is shown as The Star on the first Ordinance Survey carried out in about 1796. Blunts was not in existence as a named hamlet then. All farms used to have a number of living-in single men working for them, known as "chaps". Holwood being a large farm had more than usual of this type of employee, and some had to be boarded out, and were boarded at The Star. Regular customers at the hostelry were the wagoners who were travelling between Holwood and the docks at St Germans or Tideford. In the 1800s the road sweepings from Plymouth, which included a large amount of horse manure as well as vegetable waste from the street markets, were shipped out by barge, and bought by the landowners for distribution on the land as fertilizer. To save the long journey to the cross roads and the trip down a very rough Holwood lane, with the built in risk of damaged wheels, and then out to the fields, the wagons would drive through the village and across Bladders field, and then direct to the field where the load of fertilizer was required. That was the reason for the wide road-like path across Bladders.

With the introduction and growing Wesleyan movement, with their "total abstinence" policy, Public Houses began to become less prosperous and many in the area closed down. Those that did not close did such poor trade that many were put up for sale. When this happened, it is said that well-off Wesleyans bough them and closed them down, and turned them into houses. At one time there were eight parishes in the area with no public house, although they were still flourishing in the towns of Liskeard, Callington and Saltash.

However things came to a head in 1845. In Callington there was mass unemployment and disease, including Cholera due to poor housing conditions. Severe shortages of even basic food including corn forced the price of bread up to 1/3 d. a loaf, far beyond the reach of most people. The townsfolk living in the poorer areas of the town started to riot. They were joined by miners and other workers from the surrounding areas, who had marched on the town amid rumours of corn being stored in the Market. When it was explained to the gathering crowd that large amounts of corn were used to produce their beer, leaving none for bread, 300 Callington miners swore to give up drinking for six months to allow time for stocks to recover. Hundreds of men in the area gave up drinking completely, and it was passed on through families for many generations. This was the death knell for many village public houses. Some public houses took a long time to close completely, especially in the rural areas, but trade gradually declined and although The Star hung on as a lodging house and pub for many years, it eventually closed around 1865.

CHAPTER 13 – TIME FOR SCHOOL

When it was time to send me to School there was a choice of schools that I could attend, all two and a half miles away, and the only way of getting to these were by walking – both ways. All the children from Holwood Farm workers cottages went to Quethiock School.

It was a very lonely road with very few houses along the way. The main advantage lay in the travel arrangements for very young pupils. For many years it had been the custom to keep a disused pram behind the well at the entrance to Holwood Lane. The pram couldn't be taken all the way to Holwood every day, the road surface was far too rough. For the trip to school, a rope was attached to the front axle and manned by two older children, while the handles were in the charge of a senior pupil. When any of the very young felt that the long walk was too much for them, help was not far away.

Landrake was ruled out, as once more it was a very lonely road, with very few houses along the way. The only other children from our area to attend was the girl from next door, and she rode with her father in the mornings and stayed with relatives until he picked her up in the evening.

So it had to be Tideford Nation School. It was still two and a half miles of lonely roads, although there was a hamlet at Tideford Cross where our grandmother lived, and only about a mile from the school. After that there was only one farm beside the road, before reaching home.

The name Tideford National came from the mid nineteenth century, when the Government of the day paid 50% of the cost of building schools where none existed, providing the community contributed the other 50% and undertook the running costs and maintenance. St Luke's Church came to the rescue of Tideford and played a large part in the running of the school.

I didn't mind the journey to school too much. I knew the road to Tideford Cross very well, and when you know a road it doesn't seem too far. Before I was old enough to go to school my father strapped me into a wicker child seat, and put me on the handlebars of his bike on Sunday mornings, for a hair-raising ride to see his mother and father.

Right up to the time he died Grandfather Olding always referred to me as "Little Boy". He was a very slim man who worked on the farm at Cutcrew. He loved his horses, just like my father, and they would talk about them for hours. Granny Olding was always dressed in the old Victorian style clothes that were from her period. She seemed to glide from one room to the next, and I often used to wonder if she had any feet under that long black dress that only just came above the floor level. Even early mornings she had her little white mop cap on the top of her head, and a small, crisp spotless white apron over her dress.

On Sunday morning visits I was set in the window seat of their cottage and was given saffron cake and through the summer months, homemade lemonade. Granny Olding was always busy travelling through from the back kitchen with meat and vegetables to roast in the shining black stove that was the only source of heating in the house. One thing they never went short of was food.

I got to know that road very well over the years, especially a couple of hedges where we failed to get around corners.

Tideford School appeared to be a huge building, in my early years, but it wasn't large at all really. It was situated high up on a bank next to the Church, with the playground on three sides. Mr. Lewis the headmaster lived in the schoolhouse next to the school.

The building was entered through a lobby in the front of the building, where there were pegs on the wall for the whole school, to hang coats, hats, and dinner bags. Straight ahead was the junior section, with small long desks with attached seating forms. I think that each form held six children. There were holes in the front for inkwells, but I don't ever recall Miss Drown (later Mrs. Tebb when she married the coalman), being brave enough to supply five and six year olds with the crude wooden dip pens and ink that were standard issue for the whole school. As far as I can remember, we only had a framed slate and chalk, before graduating to pencil and paper. The remainder of the school was one large room that was divided into two by a wooden screen with glass panels at the top. Miss Taylor had one classroom, and Mr. Lewis the Senior's classroom.

Both of these classrooms were equipped with long desks seating six people. The seat and desktops were held together by cast iron frames, which would give your knees a nasty knock when you were getting in and out. For stacking away, or if seating only was required, the desktop could be swung back, over and to the rear of the seat. When the inkwells had not been removed first Mr. Lewis got very upset. If the number of ink stains on the desks were any indication of past events, the inkwells had been forgotten many times.

Two large Tortoise stoves heated the large room, and a smaller one heated the small classroom. Those large stoves were also used for heating pasties for all the children that lived too far away to get home for dinner. The lucky ones got their pasties on a thin tray on the top, while the others were arranged around the sides. There were occasions when the stove became warmer than usual, and the smell of burning would come from the pasties on the top. During the winter months, wet outdoor clothing had to be found room to dry off, again for those children who lived a distance from the school.

Milk (1/3 of a pint for each child) was introduced to school after a couple of years. It did give us a drink during the day, but gave the additional problem of finding space around the Tortoise to warm the milk for anybody that needed it warmed. The choking fumes of freshly added coke would fill the room early in the morning, and milk would sometimes get wasted from a pushed in bottle top (we had cardboard bottle tops with a perforated disc to push down to get a drinking straw in) or a bottle would get too hot and break.

The school bell would ring at five minutes to nine each morning, and thankfully it could be heard quite a distance away. It's surprising how far a young pair of legs can travel in five minutes when the thought of Mr. Lewis with his cane threatened latecomers. He had a flexible cane that he was not afraid to use, and all those tales that if you put hair on your hand, or pulled your hand downwards as he was about to strike, just didn't work. Any tricks only ended up with extra strokes of the cane, usually in the area where you couldn't even see the cane coming down.

The school wasn't particularly noted for its high quality of teaching but was well thought of as a place where pupils would get a good all round basic education. Apart from the three "R's" that formed most of the class work in the school we had very few diversions.

From about eight years old the boys, and quite a few of the girls, spent one afternoon a week on basketwork. Mr. Lewis would cut out the wooden base for canes to be added to make plant potholders or teapot stands, and for the more experienced pupils, trays. Drilling all those little holes in the plywood base with a bradawl was a tiresome job that no one seemed to want, and there was no short cut. Although it was supposed to be done over a large flat piece of wood and not over desks, its surprising how many holes appeared in the top of the desks, and your own of course. All the canes had to be cut to the correct length and put to soak, before they could be used, and even them some of them were hard to bend and twist. Over the years, some very nice trays came home from school, it must be admitted.

As a diversion, Mr. Lewis got hold of the plans to make a Tudor Village from stiff cardboard. We were all given a house to make and shown how to mark out all the pieces, ready for cutting. Between the whole school we had about four Stanley type knives to use in turns to cut all the pieces with. I remember that the glue to stick it all together with came in a pot that had to be warmed in hot water, and the glue seemed to get everywhere. The whole project took about two years to complete but it did make a fine model, of which Mr. Lewis was justly proud.

Many years later when I went back to the school to his retirement presentation, the model was still on display in the glass-fronted cupboard where the Tideford branch of the County Library was housed.

Many odd projects came around schools in those days. One that I remember well was the "Clean Hands Brigade" where we had to wash our hands thoroughly about five times a day in warm water and use Lifebuoy Soap, to get a badge at the end of, I think, one month. This was fine, but there were one or two problems. At school we did have a tap but that was all, no washbasin, the water just ran down and splashed on the floor. How does a fellow wash hands and hold a bar of soap at the same time? And who was going to carry a bar of soap to school anyway? We all ended up at the end of the allotted time with badge though.

At the field gates just above the school that now leads to a housing estate, there was often someone with a leaflet to take home when we left school in the afternoon. A bundle of woollen clothes or something similar would be exchanged for a goldfish the next morning if you brought those things along.

Just above this gate was the yellow and black triangular sign of the Automobile Association, warning drivers of a school ahead. This enamel sign was well and truly chipped. In my days it was a natural target for boys with catapults on the way home from school, and made a ringing sound when you scored a direct hit.

In 1934 the boys in the school were treated to a look at the new car Mr. Lewis had bought. Until that time he had been the proud owner of a black and green Morris Minor. Now he was the proud owner of one of the very first Morris 8's, all shining in red and black. Every fine dinnertime from now on, he would have a quick meal and then push the car out of the garage beside his house and set about cleaning and polishing his new toy. Boys were always invited to help push the car back into the garage, but "Keep your sticky fingers on the bumper, nowhere else".

Tideford village was quite large for a Cornish village. It boasted a good-sized Post Office cum village store. Butcher Congdon's shop, a drapers shop, a little sweet shop, convenient to the school, another sweet shop and grocery store on the road to St Germans, run by the Haddy family, who also ran a couple of taxis and a few lorries which were on contract to the local Council.

During the dinner hours all the children had to leave the school premises so we found all the little places to while away an hour. Sometimes a big longer......... sometimes a lot longer. Bridge Road was a very old coach road that led to a medieval bridge across the River Tiddy and on to the old road to St Germans. Many a happy hour was passed away under that bridge, with a part of a rabbit skin attached to a stick with a line on it. We were after eels. Once an eel got its teeth entangled in the fur of a rabbit skin it was trapped and couldn't escaper, or so the theory went. How you get the eels to take the skin as bait I have never found out. Still many eels did get brought out of the river by various means, mostly to slither away back within minutes.

Immediately over the bridge was a very pretty little lodge at the entrance to the Port Elliot estate, occupied by Mr. and Mrs. Stephens and their daughter Mary, who went to school at the same time as Ray and myself.

Beside the road and set back into the hedge was one of the many drinking water wells in this area. These wells were fed by springs that supplied a never ending supply of pure fresh water, which householders would just dip out with their water buckets. This well was a little bit special, it always had newts on the mossy sides, a sure sign that the water was pure, or so it was said.

Just a little way along the old road was a couple of tree trunks forming a bridge to the Island in the middle of the river. A real place for an adventure, and getting clothes torn, dirty and a sure introduction to the cane for being late back to school. Another attraction on this old road was the number of conkers lying on the ground, just waiting to be collected.

A War memorial was erected at the crossroads in the village, about 1933. It took the form of a small garden with shrubs and a Bus Shelter. A message was passed to the school that it was not for the use of school children as a playground. This rule was strictly enforced for a week or two, but the village worthies who took it upon themselves the task of enforcing the rule soon gave up. That gave us a very useful spot to carry out our games of marbles or whatever else we wanted to do, and in the dry.

Many years previously Tideford Quay was a busy place, with boats coming up the River Tiddy, to load stone from the nearby quarry and transport it to Plymouth for road building. The River Tiddy was tidal almost up to the village centre, but by the time I went to school the working quay and the boats had disappeared and the riverbed was silted up. The once fast flowing River Tiddy was reduced to a much smaller river between two banks of thick mud. Now it seems little more than a stream.

In those days the Church burial ground that was in use ran along one side of the school playground, with a pathway running from the corner of the playground towards the rear entrance to the Church. There were black iron railings on the Cemetery side and a stone wall on the Church side. At the end of this path it joined the lane that served Tideford Farm. The double doors that served the rear entrance to the Church grounds met this path and lane at a corner that we considered a natural arena. Mr. Lewis didn't like fights or even friendly playful fights. He said that they always turned into the real thing if someone hit too hard. Conkers were not popular either. Nobody seemed to pick up the disused bits of demolish conker that were left lying around.

In this arena we would have all our pretend boxing matches with all the great fighters of the day taking part. Len Harvey and Tommy Farr were always there with Joe Loude. Conkers were damaged and left lying around with no one to complain. Real fights were always popular. Half the school would turn up for that, girls included. There were often so much cheering and noise going on that the whistle that was blown when dinnertime was over was often not heard. Sometimes it was heard but fell on ears that did not want to hear.

Then Mr. Lewis would have his say.

The local boys that lived locally had an advantage here. If they knew they were late it was better not to turn up at all, have an afternoon off, no one would query that. Those of use who had coats and dinner bags in the school had no option but to go in and face the music. Or in many cases, not to face it, you just knew where it was going to land.

The old quay was built for boys' adventures, with plenty of space and nobody to say you were making too much noise. There was still the remains of a boat in the "dock" but it was now a rotting hulk. That doesn't really matter when you are young, and as one of my friends, Archie Jelly, lived in the house on the old jetty he knew which parts were safe to go into. Or so he said.

The Quay area was a wonderful place to explore, a large open space with lots of old cranes left rusting where they once worked. At one end the Riverside Garage was set up, and a couple of old cars had been thrown away in an old dock by the side of the garage. At low tide you could get to these cars and slide into another world. Mother would usually smell it before I got inside the door.

The Riverside Garage is still there, but a much larger establishment, the dock has been filled in and the garage extended over it.

Like all small places, there appears to be one family name that appears everywhere. At Blunts it was Jane. Tideford was dominated by the name of Govett. They ran the Post Office, and the haberdashery and draper store, the local Council had a couple of Govetts and the Church would be short of helpers if there were no Govetts.

The journey to and from school was always a bit of an adventure, with so many things to see and yarns to swap with all the people that were met up with on the journey. When we left home early in the morning, Mr. Searl's youngest daughter, Leolin (Leo) a couple of years older than myself was usually the first person I met. Half a mile down the hill that for some obscure reason was always called Roosta Hill, and after passing those lovely beech trees set high up on a bank, we met Molly Lansley. She lived in the farm beside the road, Trehurst. Again, she was about two years older.

Next, at Trenance Lane end, Agnes Edwards would join us. She lived at Trenance Farm, a very modern farm for those days. It even had a specially built garage, with a pit for repairs. The Sales description when the farm was offered for sale in 1919 stated that the building could also be used as a fine trap house. It was the only farm that could boast such a desirable addition. Traps or any vehicles that a farmer might have in those days were normally kept under an open fronted building at best. This fine building at Trenance Farm had tall folding doors with glass panes in the top. Painted black of course, as all doors seemed to be in those days.

At Luccombe land end, just a short distance down the road from Trenance, the Gimblett family would meet up with the growing crowd. The Gimbletts were a large family, some much older, but with only one exception, all worked on the family farm. Lucy, Gerald, Betty and Gordon went to school. Mona, Mary and Jack were at home on the farm, with Rosie and Pansy not yet started school.

The little group was joined a little further along the road by the young son of one of the Delbridge family from the farm at Trewolsta, who was always accompanied by his nursemaid. The Courts family joined us at the junction with Bones Lane at Tideford Cross. There were four of five of them, but I cannot recall their names. Next came the two Kitt boys. I remember they had flaming red hair, like their mother. Three of the Lake children joined us at the same road junction. Tideford Cross saw the last additions to our little crocodile of children. Three of the Carhart family, of which I can only remember the name of Tom, plus Tom Richard, Annie and Kathleen Heath with their younger brother

Charlie, Anne Titford, Harry, Douglas and Myrtyl Worth, with Jack Pound, completed the "outside children" from our area.

As you can imagine, there was a lot of chatter, a lot of arguments and a few fights. We all travelled complete with a "Dinner Bag".

Every week a butcher from Plymouth by the name of Wathan called on Gran Olding. There was some family connection, but I am not sure what the connection was. The little Jowett van that was used, according to the advertisements of the day, was really the last word in performance and road holding. The van was driven by Ivor, the son of the family, and I recall that he had a very bad stammer. His rounds took him through Blunts so he used to offer us a ride. We accepted once. Never again. We would rather walk and get wet through than ride with that mad man again. The Jowett van was lower to the ground and faster than anything that we had ever met before, but it certainly put us off riding with him. Up to that time we had lived by mother's theory that "third class riding was better than first class walking".

Walking home was usually a leisurely affair. If Mr. Lewis had sent me down to the little sweet and tobacconist shop near the school, run by a Mr. Perry, for his packet of twenty Players, chances were that he had given me a shilling (5 new pence) and he would give me the half penny change. Two trips to the shop would give a whole penny to spend, all at once. With a bit of luck you could find someone else with a penny to spend and you could buy a little paper sleeve with five Woodbines inside, plus of course the picture stiffener, usually known as a "Fag card" - very collectable and much in demand.

There was no trouble finding a quiet enough spot to have a smoke of your share of the packet on the way home. Unused cigarettes would be packed away in a full sized cigarette packet and stowed away in a wall behind a loose stone, to be retrieved at a later date.

If the weather was a bit chilly when we set out in the mornings, we would warm up by taking a hoop part of the way to school. Girls would take a skipping rope. A hoop could be used quite safely on our roads, the chances of a runaway hoop running into a car was almost non-existent.

An iron hoop with a snake bar was the favourite. The snake bar was an iron bar about eighteen inches long, with a twist on one end that resembled a snake, but only about two inches long. One curve would be used to push the hoop along while the inner curve would hold it back going down hills. Those thin iron hoops would certainly run fast, but occasionally the nice ringing sound that they made would suddenly stop as it hit a stone or other obstruction. You knew then that you had to go and talk to Mr. Buller the blacksmith to get a repair.

Mr. Buller always got the work. He only charged tuppence. Bill Jane charged a penny more. It was at times like this that wooden hoops came out that had to be hit with a stick, and held back by getting the stick on the inside. The old rim of a bicycle wheel made a substitute at times, they could be pushed by a stick in the centre groove, but were very heavy and wouldn't steer very well. We were not allowed to take hoops into the school as it was built on a high bend, and Mr. Lewis couldn't risk runaway hoops tearing down the village street, so we took ours as far as Tideford Cross and left them there for the day.

We didn't see much in the way of accidents with cars, there were so few on the road. There were a couple of occasions when we came across cars and vans that had lost a wheel. Morris Cowleys and light vans were the usual victims. There were more of these than anything else, and loosing wheel nuts and wheels were a regular occurrence. Some cars and light vans had tyres fitted to detachable rims that were in turn clamped to the wooden spokes.

It was not unusual to come across one of these where there were bends in the road especially at the end of a slope where the cars had picked up a bit of speed. When the rim flew off, the wooden spokes would part break off as they came in contact with the road. One such spot where there were a few incidents over the years was at Kilquite Lane end, but that lane end was memorable to us because of the wild garlic that grew there. On one side of the road was a small passing place in the road, on the other side a low bank about twenty feet long that each year was filled with the evil smelling stuff. Pity, because the white flower was quite attractive.

There were flowers of every description on the road. Each month of the year brought it's own varieties, and we got to know exactly where they would be. Luccumbe Lane, leading to the Gimbletts farm always seemed what a lane should be. A soft patch of green grass right down the centre made walking a pleasure. On each side were tracks with potholes filled with hard core, where the cart and wagon wheels cut their own path in any soft spots. There was no room for anyone else, a cart would fill the lane.

Hedges would fill up in rotation with foxgloves, wild orchids, wood anemones, violets, bluebells and vigorous clumps of primroses. Wild honeysuckle would force its way through the branches that would in turn produce little white flowers which in turn became delicious blackberries, to be picked and added to apple, and be served up in the form of a pie, with thick cream of course.

Primroses were normally sweet smelling small yellow flowers, but this was one place where there was something different. Over the hedge, in the corner of the first field down the lane, were pink primroses, not all that unusual in this part of the world. One secret place in this field a collection of dark purple and even almost jet-black primroses grew which was very unusual. I am told on good authority that they still bloom in the same spot

The lane into Trenance was a different matter. Since it had been purchased by the Council in 1919 the road had been made up and the hedgerows were so well trimmed that there was not much in the way of flowers to grow. The hedges always got pared (trimmed) just at the time when mother nature would begin the unending job of distributing the seeds of wild flowers for the following year. When you live in the country, hedges become important, and although boys will sometimes get a bit destructive, we were always taught to treat hedges with respect.

CHAPTER 14 – HEDGES, LANES AND TREES

A good Cornish hedge is a work of art. The stones are slotted together to make all sorts of patterns. Straight lines of regular shaped stones, herring bone patterns, or a mixture of both (known as Jack and Jill pattern), are to be found everywhere. These stone hedges should last a lifetime. Of course there were just ordinary farm hedges too, compared to the pure stone hedges. After a few years, nature would find plants and grass that would clothe the entire surface of the hedge and make it a suitable hedge for climbing. Just around the corner at Blunts, on the Tideford road, there was a stone hedge around the road corner of Mr. Lansley's field. When it was built someone with wisdom had placed five extra long, flat stones lying horizontally at intervals of 45 degrees on the road side of the hedge. I don't know what the original purpose was, but they made a convenient spot to be able to walk along and walk to the top of the hedge. I assume they were intended as either mounting stones for horses, or as mounting steps for high-seated wagonettes.

We could always find slow worms, lizards, shrews and a few dormice in our travels, they all make their homes in the hedges. A good hedge was a vital link in the food chain of our wild life, and in those days for the villagers too. There was a plentiful supply of rabbits to feed many a family in the village. To keep the kestrels circling overhead well supplied with food for their young, were plenty of mice and lizards. Foxes, stoats and weasels all relied on a new family of rabbits coming along every few weeks. A handclap at any field gate would produce dozens of little white tails, scampering for a safe refuge at the base of the hedge. Birds are assured of a plentiful supply of berries, Rose hips and the purple fruits of the ivy, with holly berries for the blackbirds.

Holly was always used as Christmas trees in the rural areas, because holly and ivy were reputed to have strange powers that would keep the Goblins away until the New Year. There was the added bonus that holly as well as being decorative, was available.......and free.

There were always lanes and woods to explore, both on the school route or just around the village. Some farmers were not too keen to have boys around their land, but there were means of getting around any objections that they had. A farmer by the name of Stephens had a smallholding (now demolished) on the Landrake side of Blunts, next to Bearah farm. His land included Bearah woods, and in his woods were some lovely chestnut trees that produced the sweetest chestnuts around. We were always brought up to ask for anything before taking it, even if it was only some wild flowers, if they were on someone else's property. Ray and I walked a long way to ask Mr. Stephens if we could have some chestnuts. Imagine our surprise when he said "NO".

After that we always took the short cut to his chestnut trees with a good-sized bag, and took our fill. Then we would go and ask if we could have some, to which he would always give the same answer. A few years later he told father that he had two very good children, who always asked before going on his land, and didn't argue when refused. Comments such as this really made the halos glow for an hour or two.

Not only the wildlife found something of interest, humans found their requirements as well. In my young days, some of the older generation would find all the herbs they needed for their aches and pains, as well as cures for anything from a headache to boils, all growing for free in the hedges. Hazel nuts were always a valuable fruit of the hedgerow, if you could find them before the squirrel. A good hazel nut bush had to be kept secret from neighbours too, they might pick them before they were fully ripe (August 22nd, St Filbert's Day was the date that they should be ripe), and ripen them off in a dry shed.

Crab apples and wild cherries were always gathered to make jams. Blackberries were fine too, but had to be gathered at the correct time of the year. Country folk reckon that on Michaelmas Day, Satan got thrown out of Heaven and he went out and spit on all the blackberries. Since that time, all blackberries loose their taste on Michaelmas Day, and nobody picks them, but leave them there for the birds. Then there was the mistletoe that was gathered as a sure guarantee of fertility.

The woods at Holwood and Bearah supplied a good supply of dry wood for fires and leaf mould for the gardens of the farm workers, as well as being a wonderland for boy's games. What better place was there to surprise the enemy than from the top of a tree?

Gamekeepers had private reserves on the edges of woods where they kept their precious supplies of young pheasants and partridge for the annual shoots for their employers and friends, between October and February. No unaccompanied boys were allowed near them. These reserves were well protected by strings holding tins with an odd stone to act as a rattle, to either warn the gamekeeper or frighten any intruder.

Poachers did get into the woods at night to take home a special meal of pheasant or anything else that was going, but the gamekeeper was always around, or so it seemed. I don't really know when they slept. Although gamekeepers seemed to know most things that were going on, there were things they didn't know. They were always grateful and would always reward any boy that found a pheasant's nest with eggs.

There were at times, especially on a Saturday afternoon a few farmhands and young men from other villages around, usually with a few dogs. On one occasion, when I asked what they were going to do, I didn't get much of a reply. When I asked at home I was told not to go anywhere near them. That to me was an invitation to find out. I just stayed by one of the men that I knew slightly and nobody took much notice of me. It looked as though I was with him. We went into Mr. Stephen's wood and a lot of examination of holes in the ground went on. Everybody had a good smell of the holes, and eventually it was decided which was to be the right one.

Up to this stage I was completely bewildered by what was going on, but dare not show my ignorance by asking. Then some of the small terrier dogs were put into the holes, to he replaced by other dogs when the first one's reappeared. There was a lot of talking and a lot of shh...ing while the self appointed leader's listened. After what seemed an eternity, picks and shovels were produced from sacks, and men started digging away the front of the holes.

Then I knew what it was all about. A poor badger came to the opening with one of the dogs firmly gripped by its neck. A large pair of what I can only describe as pincers, were used to drag the badger out into the open. This I thought would be the end, and I couldn't see much in it as a sport. Not far away a round kind of circle had been made with some fallen tree trunks. The badger was forced into a sack and dragged to this arena, where it was tipped out on the ground. The dogs were all barking and straining at the ropes that held them, as if they know what was to come, maybe as some sort of reward.

What took place next I cannot describe. What pain that badger must have suffered when the bogs were let in two at a time, to terrify and fight the poor animal that was so badly injured that it could not start to defend itself.

I couldn't stay and longer and ran home. But what could I do? I needed to tell someone what I had seen but I had strict instructions not to go anywhere near those men and their dogs.

Charlie Jane the gamekeeper was the only one around that I could trust. When I told him what I had seen he gave me a pat on the head and told me to go home and not worry about it. He would take care of everything. He took his double barrel shotgun off the wall and walked towards the end of the village.

A few days later the village was talking about the incident where Charlie had come across a gang of badger baiters, and had shot the badger to put it out of its misery. I never saw or heard any more men with dogs in our area again.

In those days badger baiting was not illegal, although it was generally frowned upon. Fox hunting and otter hunting were different. The hunt meets were always well advertised in the local papers and were well attended. Otter hunting was confined to the upper reaches of the River Tiddy, and the River Lynhar around Pillaton, but was losing popularity as the otters became more scarce. No hunt saboteurs around then.

With so much wild life around there was no need for foxes to go anywhere near a house to forage for food, as today. All they needed was there to help themselves to. They did come around the fowl's houses at night though, to see if there was a spare meal going. The trouble with foxes was that they could get into a fowl's house and just have fun, killing all the fowls and leave without taking any away.

There were some wonderful trees around our village that gave all boys a lot of pleasure. On the opposite side of the road from the Chapel were three mature beech trees that for generations had given the lads with a pocket knife a good place to practice their woodcutting, and a convenient place to declare their undying love for some of the local girls.

One of the trees had a large branch that would allow a rope for a swing, that could swing you right out over the hedge and the path field. Two of them had branches low enough to get a grip to start you climbing. Getting down was sometimes a bit of a problem. This was always a favourite place to play, even without the swinging rope.

On the opposite side of the road from our house were three tall beech trees on the bank that formed the hedge of our field. The branches were too high up for us to reach to do much in the way of climbing. Anyway you don't want to be seen climbing trees, right outside your own door where parents can see what's going on. When autumn came around the leaves would all turn brown and when the wind blew they made a kind of lovely friendly rattling sound. The rest of the year they were clothed in all their green finery that would turn over to show a different colour when the wind blew.

Half way down Roosta Hill were four more very tall beech trees. Growing high up on a very wide hedge, they were a bit difficult to get to, but we managed somehow. I think the most exciting part of climbing up to these trees was the lovely slide down to the road. It always left a mark, and a sharp-eyed mother always noticed. There were times that the descent was a little quicker than intended, and we would end up with an odd graze or cut. Why did mothers always consider that Iodine was good for cuts and grazes, and paint it on at every opportunity? The stuff would sting like mad, and we would try to avoid it if possible. There were times when the little fluted bottle could not be found.

The trees on either side of the kissing gates at the lower end of Bladders Field on the way to Holwood were large and well clothed in leaves. They had escape routes that could be used on either side of the hedge to gain a good start if needed. Many a boy, and girls too, have been thankful to be able to chose which side of the hedge to come down to earth, when an ill timed giggle had been heard by the wrong person.

At Holwood Farm, just two fields away, all the workers cottages were built among giant beech trees, with a row of elms at the rear. Those elms would be full of rooks and crows, all squabbling over food and nests. You would hardly believe the noise birds can make. It would all come to a peak when the young had been hatched and were making their first trips away from the nests.

With all the trees around, we should never have suffered with a cold if all the old wives tales could be believed. It was said that if you could get leaves to fall on you before they reached the ground, you would be free of colds for the winter.

CHAPTER 15 – THE SEASONS

When you are a small lad, you don't really take a great deal of notices of the changing seasons. It's just as if everything seems to change when it is supposed to. Mr. Lansley was a very hard working and methodical farmer. His farm at Trehurst was always kept clean and tidy, even the farmyard seemed to be clear of the mud and smelly slime that was normal at other farms. All his gates hung correctly and his implements were always put away after use, cleaned and oiled, ready for when next required, all the sort of things that every other farmer meant to do, but rarely carried out.

Beside Roosta Hill was the one field in the district that always seemed to act as a calendar. One day, early in the year, Mr. Lansley would take his horse out to that field and start to plough. Then you knew that it was spring. This was a steep field, but considered to be an ideal place for root crops, flowers and vegetables. It was well drained and "out of wind and into sun", was the local way of describing such a field.

The ploughing had to be done with a light turn over plough, so that all the furrows could be turned up the hill. Most of the leases given out to farmers by the land owners of those days would stipulate which fields could be ploughed and how much lime and dung had to be fed to each field, and how often.

Mr. Lansley had a routine with this field where, because of the steepness, a lot of the soil would fall to the bottom. Somehow it had to be brought to the top again. Every year, or so it seemed, he ploughed three or four furrows across the lower part of the field. Into these three or four furrows he would place a lot of sea sand and farmyard manure and the whole lot would be well worked together. Then he used what appeared to be an oversized wheelbarrow with three wheels, which he called a "butty". To this would be attached two horses, and the butty was filled with the rich soil. The load would be driven to the top of the field, and turned on its side, to which was fitted a stout skid. As the horses were driven across the top, the soil would be pulled out of the Butty, to replace the soil that had slipped down the field. This was the only time that I can recall seeing one of these implements used, but I understand that they were quite popular in other areas, like the Tamar Valley where there was cultivation on steep lands.

Very soon it would be ploughing time for everyone. Ploughing seemed to start in spring and still be going on in the autumn. It was a very slow process; usually five days work to plough a five-acre field. Today with a tractor it is only a few hours work.

People nowadays walk for exercise and relaxation. Pity the pour ploughman with two, maybe more, horses walking behind a plough all day, looking at the rear end of a horse. With one foot in a furrow and the other six inches higher on the unploughed land, while all the time making adjustments to the depth and width of the furrow being ploughed.

The ploughman and horses were constantly followed by a flock of hungry screeching seagulls, all sweeping around in a never-ending spiral, looking for worms and grubs that the plough would uncover. Occasionally an odd gull would perch on the back of the horse as if to take a rest, but no one took much notice. The main aim of the ploughman must have been to get to the end of the furrow and look back to see that it was straight, and turn the plough around for the return journey.

For relaxation, what did the ploughman do at weekends? Enter Ploughing matches, or what we would call today, competitions. There was very keen rivalry to see who could plough the best furrow. A good ploughman and his favourite horse would work as a team, each knowing what the other expected, and it paid dividends.

At the end of the day, the whole field of ploughing would be judged and prizes awarded to the best ploughman. Such things as straight furrows, of regular depth and width, with well set up, unbroken furrows, inverted correctly to bury all traces of previous crops and trash, and expose as much soil as possible to weathering, combined with good drainage. A work of art really.

We knew then that it wouldn't be long before there would be a lot of work to be done both at home and at school. Apart from the tasks around the house that were always accepted as normal, and the jobs at school that were interpreted as school work, all work done was in no way compulsory, maybe expected, but none was forced.

At school Mr. Lewes would get all boys from about seven years old out in his so called School Garden for one afternoon a week, weather permitting, even if it was only to pull a few weeds. He always said that in return we would get some benefits in the shape of improvements to the school. One year we came back from the summer holiday to find that all the long desks had been replaced by modern desks. Each desk seated two people so you had to be a bit careful who you were sitting beside to avoid problems in class. Somehow I think that Mr. Lewis had prior knowledge of what was about to happen and used that knowledge to get some the less interesting jobs in his garden done.

The springtime hobby, on the way home from school, was finding birds nests and then keep looking in to see what was happening inside. Although hundreds of nests were found each year, and boys being destructive animals that they are, very few nests were ever damaged. The whereabouts of a nest was not normally for public knowledge, everybody found their own. The only person that was privileged to share such valuable information was Sam Dolley, the parish roadman. He had to be told in case he came along with his curved paring hook and his stick with a fork at the end and accidentally destroyed the nest, as he was trimming back the grass and brambles from the hedge.

When the young birds were leaving to fly it became almost a ritual to pick up exhausted or lost young birds and put them somewhere safe for the parent birds to find them.

Young partridges were a different matter. We would sometimes come across a hen partridge that would make a great show of being frightened with a loud screeching and pretence of trying to fly away or running around with one wing drooping as if injured. While this show was going on the young would be hurriedly finding refuge in some safe spot, to be reunited with the parent bird when all danger had passed.

Around this time we would often find a further distraction on the journey home from school. We would often meet up with a travelling Shire Stallion on his way to spend the night at one of the local farms. These were massive beasts, all shining and gaily decorated with ribbons and brass bells. Their grooms who would walk beside them for weeks at a time would add to the overall picture, by being smartly turned out with equally shiny boots and leather leggings, plus a bowler hat. Whole villages would turn out to see these fine horses pass through on their annual parade through the district.

It was around this time of year that boys could earn a bit of money to spend on Sunday School trips or save for the Christmas trip to Plymouth. Every farmer had a field or two that had a fine dashle (thistle) crop that needed to be cut by hand. To use a mower would scatter the seeds too much and next year every field would be well seeded.

My father's brother, Uncle Jim and his wife Aunt Hilda farmed quite a large farm for those days (167 acres) at Trebrown, about a mile away. He would always find me some work with a sharp paring hook, and pay the going rate for the job. ONE PENNY AND AN EGG A DAY. It was back breaking work and the days could be long. I think that the walk home was the worst part. It was almost enough to put you off going the next day. Still, it had to be done.

With a bit of luck Mr. Gerald Stevens, who had the old manor farm at Leigh, about a mile past Trebrown, would be in the village when you going his way. Perhaps it would be more truthful to say that the trip to Trebrown would try to be arranged to coincide with Mr. Stevens return to his farm. He would give a lift in his Austin Tourer car, and make a fine start to the day.

There was no such thing as pocket money in those days. I don't think the term had even been invented. At the end of the week I used to toddle off to the massive farm kitchen to be paid and do a little bargaining. I didn't really want an egg for wages so I would forfeit the eggs for a few extra pennies. I would usually end up with a special egg of some description, maybe a double yolker.

I had an offer from Mr. Libby of Bearah farm one year to cut his daisies, and he had plenty. It looked like a good thing to get involved with. Bearah wasn't too far to walk and I set off full of enthusiasm to be greeted by a blunt hook. Young boys are not too good at sharpening tools, but it was just one more lesson to be learned. For almost three weeks I remember, I almost broke my back in hot weather, before the two fields that I had to clear were free of daisies. When it was time to get paid Mr. Libby, a very tall man who seemed to naturally stoop over, and only shaved on very rare occasions, had to be somewhere else. However his wife assured me that I would be paid the very next day. What I didn't know was that Mr. Libby had a very poor memory where paying out money was concerned. As a very Christian family who always attended Chapel twice every Sunday there was no need to worry. When it came around time to go on a Sunday School trip the outstanding debt would be cleared at the seaside where it could be spent. Or so I was told........ and believed.

As a very small lad I felt conspicuous standing on the seafront at Looe, looking up to this giant of a man and asking for my wages. I think I was in disgrace for most of that day, and a few more after that, for the way I said "thank you" when he handed me the princely sum of THREE PENCE (a little above 1p). Never again did I work for Mr. Libby for a PENNY AND AN EGG.

Summer was really on the way when through the open schoolroom windows came the sound of grass machines from the fields of Mr. Creeber who lived at Tideford Farm, whose fields adjoined the school. He was always the first to start grass cutting. Once he had started, then the other farmers around would try to remember where they had last seen their own grass mowers. More often than not it would be lying where it finished work last year, with a rusty, probably broken knife still in place.

Farmers are still notorious for leaving their tools where they were last used, and oil is a waste of money if the thing is not going to be used for another year.

All over the parish, horses would be harnessed up on a fine day and placed one each side of the centre shaft. An assortment of chains, reins and whipple trees would be attached, a UVECO sack folded to form a cushion on the steel seat for the driver, and the job was ready to being. This was usually the time when thoughts would turn to spare knives, or maybe finding the files to sharpen the existing knife. The driver would sit for hours with only the rear end of two horses to talk to, or maybe to swear at just to break the monotony.

Round and around the field the mower would be driven at a steady pace. At each corner the driver would pull on the long lever beside him to lift the knife beam clear of the grass while the mover changed direction.

On the gate to the field would be one man at least sharpening a knife that was clamped to the top bar of the gate, ready to make an exchange with the one in the machine when the driver needed it. A dull edge on the knife would result in uncut grass clogging up the knife beam and a long stop to free the grass.

Many a finger was lost removing grass from the knives and steel fingers of the cutting beam. One movement from one horse and the sharp knife would move and quickly remove any human fingers in the path of the knife. Behind the machine would be laid out neat swarths of freshly cut grass ready to dry off as quickly as possible. As the grass dried on one side an army of workers would come along with pitch forks and pikes to turn it over to dry on the other side. Everybody would join in, men, women and children all had to do their share. If the hay was not to be saved until the next day, and there was any risk of rain all the grass had to be made up into "Pooks" to reduce the risk of too much grass getting wet. Next day it all had to be scattered around again to dry out completely.

The actual harvesting was hard work and it all had to be done with the weather in mind. All the dried grass was raked into long rows across the field with one man on a horse rake. That was a rattle-y contraption that almost doubled in length once it was in the field. This was achieved by fitting an extension to each end of the main section of the rake. The road wheels were then fitted to the ends, and the horse shafts swung around at right angles. A horse would be attached to each hay sweep, for small fields one sweep was usually enough. Sweeping was considered hard work. The sweep itself having, no wheels, was pulled around collecting grass from the long rows of hay that had been deposited by the rake, the forward facing tines slipping underneath the dried grass. It entailed a lot of manhandling. If the grass was dry, there were not too many problems, but grass that was not quite ready would roll under the long tines, and the sweep had to be pulled back to collect grass left behind.

At the end of the sweep, when the dried hay was brought to the point where it was going to be lifted on to the newly made hayrick, the sweep operator would lift up the handles as it was still moving. The tips of the tines would stick into the ground, and the whole sweep, complete with hay would be tipped in the right position, as the sweep did a complete somersault, and end up in a position ready to collect another load of the sweet smelling hay.

That was the theory behind the thing. If the ground was a bit soft in places, or the sweep operator came in at an angle, the sweep tines would sometimes stick into the ground too far, and the tips of the tines would break off. This would mean a trip to Bill Jane the carpenter, and maybe he had a new tine of the right length. Failing this perhaps the tine could be reshaped. If no new tines were available, perhaps a new one would be made by tomorrow....... or tomorrow........ or tomorrow.

In the farm kitchen things were going ahead to get everything ready for "drinkings". Dinner time usually meant a hot pasty, fresh from the oven, washed down with tea, hot or cold, but usually very sweet. Pasties were wrapped in greaseproof paper and then further wrapped in white cloths. There was unusually generous portions of saffron cake or maybe an apple pasty or slices of tart for afters. This was the sort of thing that held the larger farmers in good stead for future help when needed. Plenty of good food........ plenty of help.

The whole meal was delivered to the hayfield by the ladies carrying large wicker baskets covered by white cloths. The men would all sit around, like gentlemen, waiting to be served, and be passed cups of tea in china cups that were usually kept especially for such occasions. Very best behaviour was the order of the day, especially if the missus was helping out, either in the kitchens or passing food around.

There was normally a limited amount of cider available, but not a plentiful supply at this time of the day. Cider and hayfield equipment don't mix too well. At teetotal farms, no cider was available and this was fully accepted. Nobody was ever heard to complain.

The whole atmosphere was like one big picnic, the quality of the hay would be discussed, the weather prospects for the rest of the day, and the state of someone else's farm, before the pipes of baccy and Woodbines were finished and the work would start once more. Later in the afternoon there would be a further break for refreshments, seed cake and sandwiches probably, again with tea and maybe by now a drop more cider would be available.

If a pole and grab was being used to lift the hay on to a tall rick, cider did seem to make a difference to the sight of the man working the horse that lifted the grab. A grab going through the pulleys as the top of the pole had to be avoided if possible, so there was likely to be some reallocation of jobs as the day wore on, and the cider bottle became emptier. Most farmers knew who would have a fair share of the cider and would allocate jobs accordingly.

At the end of a day's harvesting there would often be a supper for all the workers, when all the problems, and the quality of the hay would be discussed before heading towards home and their own farm or smallholding with work still to be done there.

With the promise of good weather tomorrow, it would probably be a repeat of today, until all the hay in the area was safely in.

I seem to have spent a lot of time at Trebrown farm, due I suppose to the family connections and I always seemed to get on well with Uncle Jim. They had one son Bernard, who was well and truly spoiled. Aunt Hilda's family were fairly well off by normal standards of the day, and I always assumed that they were responsible for the good quality of everything at Trebrown, including the stock.

The house itself seemed to be of enormous proportions, compared to our cottage. The kitchen was huge, with a long scrubbed table down the middle. The fireplace always fascinated me. Hanging down from some unseen bars up the chimney was a collection of hooks and bars that all had a different role to play in suspending all the different kettles that were in the fireplace. There was the fountain always full of near boiling water. As the brass tap to get the hot water out was more than half way up the side, no hot water could be removed until some cold water was put into the top. That way it never ran dry.

The fire itself would take a whole faggot of wood at a time, which was often to get it going in the morning. The fire was kept going all night with a "mock" (huge log, or tree root) just smouldering away at the back of the fireplace, that only needed a blow or two with the bellows to bring the sparks into a living flame. In the huge fireplace was the normal oven, with a clome oven on the opposite side. This was an oven lined with a clay-like material. Hot embers from the fire were put inside the oven through the hinged door at the front, and left inside until the oven was hot enough to do all the baking for that day. When the oven was hot enough the embers were raked out into the fire, and the baking put into the oven on iron racks, the door closed and not opened again until the baking had been done. There were no temperature gauges or thermostats, every farm's wife knew her own oven, and that was the only gauge required.

Cousin Bernard had toys that the rest of us could only dream about. On the top of a huge glass cabinet in the large drawing room, was a collection of racing cars that we were only occasionally given a demonstration of. They were gyro powered, a thing that the rest of us children had never even seen before, and were presents from his mother's family, the Ryders from Lidcott near Haessenford. Bernard was not allowed to play with them either. He was so destructive he would get more pleasure from destroying them than playing with them.

The farm itself had some lovely old buildings and barns where you could have all kinds of games, especially when the weather was wet. Barn owls were plentiful then, there were always owls, doves and pigeons watching every corner of the farmyard even during the day. At night they would join the numerous bats that came out to collect their fill of insects as they weaved and darted every way.

At the rear of the barn there was a big mowhay that would hold six or seven large corn ricks, with plenty of room for the annual visit of the threshing machine. They had a few fields of potatoes, some swedes and mangols for feeding stock. Ducks, bantams, gleenies, guinea fowl and chickens ran all over the place, with a lot of geese that seemed to think that nipping the legs of boys in short trousers was some sort of game.

There must have been at least twenty cows to be milked twice a day, but the process to turn milk to cream was vastly different to what my mother did. First the milk was cooled, by letting it flow over a cold water filled type of radiator, or cooller. Then milk that was to be made into cream and butter would be carried into the dairy, two buckets at a time, using a wooden yoke over the shoulders, to ease the load. The dairy had a blue-slated floor with slate benches on all sides. Milk that was to be used for cream was poured into a stainless steel tank that held about three gallons fitted to a machine called a separator. There was a handle on the side that was just waiting for some boy to come along and start turning. As the handle was turned milk would come out of one spout and be directed to a churn, while out of another spout would come a thin sort of cream. That handle got harder and harder to turn, and the bell that rung every time the handle went around told the whole world when you were slowing up or stopped for a rest.

The cream was allowed to stand and gradually got thick enough to be made into butter for Mr. Ryeder to take off to Market on Wednesdays and Saturdays. The cream never did get that thick and crusty look that the cream produced by the old method achieved.

The hay harvest seemed to go on all around the area for an awful long time, and the blacksmith's shop had a long line of broken knives to be repaired with no time to spare for the essential things of life like mending broken hoops for people like me.

With the hay harvest completed and all the hay safely stacked in hayricks, farmers would start to think about corn harvest and binders. A binder appeared to be a real Heath Robinson machine at first glance. It would arrive in a field of ripe corn, drawn by two horses with a spare horse on hand to be harnessed in when the work started.

It took about an hour to remove the two travelling wheels and turn the whole thing around so that it was using a large centre wheel that had been tucked up out of sight and from now on would be used as a driving wheel. There were two large canvases to be fitted, a large ball of twine and some revolving flails. No wonder that when these machines were first imported from America the farm workers refused to work them. However when in action these cumbersome machines would cut the corn and pack it up in sheaves, put the string around it, tie the knot and throw the sheaf out of the back of the machine. Men and boys didn't have to do so much turning to dry the corn but it all had to be stood in "shocks" overnight. That meant that about five of the sheaves had to be stacked together to form a kind of wigwam to help keep the corn dry if it should rain. Not an easy task when the sheaves were taller than you.

There was real concern when the weather turned to rain and forgot to stop. The corn would start to grow again where it stood, and the straw would turn black. And the farmers would talk about it, in not very complimentary ways.

No sweeps were used in the harvesting of corn, just wagons pulled by a horse. It would drive up and down between the rows and the sheaves would be thrown on to the wagon for transporting to the Mowhay, where it would be handled straight on to the stack. There it would stay until threshing time came around later in the year, when Bill Kerslake from St Ive would be doing his rounds of the farms, with his steam driven threshing machine.

About the end of July is when the song of the birds gradually started to decline. Birds are reputed to have chosen their mate for the year by St Valentine's Day, but by the end of July they begin their annual moult, and the lack of song is their way of making themselves less conspicuous, greenfinches and doves excepted.

Up in the fields the farmers would be working out how many more weeks it would be before the potatoes would be ready for digging and that meant backache, but a few more pennies. All too soon, the weeks passed by. On the appointed day there would be sacks placed at various points up and down the field. A lot of men with hand potato diggers would be behind a plough that had been specially modified for the job, by Bullers at Pounds. As the plough went forward some of the potatoes in the row would be unearthed. The hand diggers would make sure that all the potatoes were uncovered, ready for picking up.

The plough was later replaced by a "Proper Tiddy Digger" that would "scat the b....y tiddies everywhere", father said. In more polite terms the potatoes would be scattered over a wide area with the steel claws that spun around at the rear of the machine. Women and boys had sacks tied around our necks to form a large pocket in the front. You can guess the rest. We went along picking up potatoes as we went, and put them in the waiting sacks when the pockets were full. You would never believe how many potatoes would grow in one singe row, and there were hundreds of rows in each field.

At the end of the day there was always a good meal at the farm kitchen. The potatoes? They would end up either stored in frost proof barns, or buried in straw lined pits and well covered with straw and earth, to be opened up again, probably not until early the next year, when all other sources of potatoes will have been exhausted. Uncle Jim never forgot to say thank you for your work, and never forgot to add up how much he owed you. What is more important, he never forgot to pay.

I suppose that I must have enjoyed the hard work, or did it just to make me feel that I was as good as anyone else at taking on my share of the work. Whatever it was I was always around for more.

There was always time left over for the rest of life's little pleasures, like getting a few apples from the orchard of Mr. Pote at Old Barn. Sometimes there was time to get ill and recover before I got home to face the music. Father was easy going in some ways, but he was very strict about some things, and stealing apples was one of them.

Eventually the day would arrive when Bill Kerslake and his threshing outfit would arrive at Trebrown. At that time I don't think there was anyone else who travelled around the district with a steam engine and threshing machine. Combine harvesters where corn cutting and threshing were done with one machine didn't come to Cornwall until after the Second World War.

The steam engine would be manoeuvred into place with the pink and red coloured thresher lined up in front of it. The two were connected by a long belt from the outside flywheel of the engine to the pulley wheel by the side of the thresher. After what seemed hours, the blocks were all in position against the traction engine wheels, and against the thresher wheels, to stop any movement. Sacks at the ready to collect the grain, men in position to throw sheaves from the stack of corn to the men who would feed the thresher, and men to collect the sheaves of straw after it had been threshed. Then when all was ready, there would be a blast on the steam whistle and the engine would give a few hearty chuff..........chuff's as if impatient to get moving. The thresher would turn over and within a few minutes that monotonous drone would settle down to be heard all day.

Straw would be spilled out at one end, all bundled up ready to be stacked on its own to be used as bedding for stock. At the rear of the thresher three or four sacks would be hung in place to collect the grain that had been threshed from the corn. It was a full time job for someone to remove these sacks when they were full and replace them with empty sacks.

No mention yet of boy's work? Don't worry, it was coming. When the straw is separated from the grain inside this droning monster, full of wheels and pulleys, there are all the ears of corn that held the grain to find a home for.....somewhere. All these ears came out with the rest of the dust that is always present with corn, just in front of the sacks being filled with grain. It was boy's jobs to keep the area clear from this "Douse". That was a filthy job, the ears of corn would go in around your neck, and creep everywhere. It would get in your hair and socks and generally made you feel dirty and uncomfortable. Still you were treated as an equal when it came time for pasties and drinkings, and the money was good, A PENNY AND AN EGG.

All the dogs would be standing by as the stacks of corn got lower, waiting for their turn to earn their keep. Although the stacks had not been in place very long, rats would have made themselves at home, and they were soon going to have to look for a new home. That's why all the men tied their trousers with a bit of binder twine, just below the knee. Rats would run anywhere when chased by a dog.

Some of those dogs were so very quick when it came to catching rats. The little terriers would appear to be able to give a rat a quick shake to stun them and collect another in its mouth while their mouth was open to drop the first one. Our little Nell was always considered a good ratter.

Dogs on farms were divided into two, farm dogs and house dogs. The farm dogs knew their place and their job. They normally lived outdoors all year and would find shelter in a barn or maybe a kennel in a sheltered spot. But they were always well fed and cared for. House dogs were allowed into the house, but the were still working dogs, and when the master got up, so did the dog.

Looking back, we always had a lot to do, but never had time to look after the angora rabbits that we kept beside the shipon at Blunts. Father or mother usually had to feed them and clean their hutch. I wonder why?

All too fast summer sunshine would get weaker, and all the

wonderful sights and smells of summer would be replaced by the more down to earth smell of autumn. The day would come when all the farm horses and carts would be brought into the farmyard, and the dung heap would be disturbed. The carts would be loaded and driven off to the fields where mounds of the so called, healthy, smelling stuff would be deposited in neat rows, ready for the men to come along and distribute it over the field. All over the area, windows would be tightly closed. Farmers called it giving the fields their winter dressing.

The run up to Christmas was a busy time at Trebrown Farm. Poultry for the dinner table of the people living in Plymouth had to be killed and plucked and sent off to market in plenty of time. One of the buildings would be set aside for all the ladies who would pluck all the feathers off the chicken, geese, ducks and turkeys. They would sit around on an assortment of stools and seats, with aprons and headscarves, and pluck away all day and sometimes well into the night. For some of them it was a good chance to have a good chat with neighbours that they rarely saw. After plucking, all the poultry was cleaned and trussed up with fine white string and lined up in the dairy on those cold slate benches. Mr. Ryder took most of them off to market with the eggs, butter and cream, while others went to local butchers, and a few went to the locals who had done some favours, or were in need.

Of course Christmas was one part of the year that no boy would ever forget, no matter how the seasons slipped by. It was not the season of big parties and lots of presents in those days. There were presents of course, but it was usually restricted to one major toy, the rest being made up with oranges and nuts in the Christmas stocking with a few cheap books, a ball, and family games as an extra.

The house would be decorated and the "front room" fire lit, with a real holly tree covered in tinsel. We did have lights on the tree, small coloured candles in clip on holders were lit, but under strict supervision. Many weeks before Christmas a special fowl or cockerel had been selected and fattened up ready for our Christmas dinner. Christmas was usually a quiet time in our village, just a lot of coming and going between neighbours. Boxing Day was special, when we all went off to Trebrown.

By tradition Boxing Day was devoted to rabbiting. All around the area, there would be men, boys, dogs, nets and guns all setting off for a day's sport. All farmers knew which hedge was going to provide most sport, and at the same time get rid of some of the hungry uninvited guests that were eating large proportions of the crops. Ferrets would be sent down holes and nets placed over the remaining holes. With luck, rabbits would come scampering out to take their chance against dogs and shotguns. It's surprising how many times they succeeded. There would be hot drinks brought to the fields during the morning, just when the remains of the previous day's turkey would be demolished, plus some extras, specially made for the day.

There would be a lot of chatter and well wishing, with probably one or two deals or arrangements made, before all the rabbits caught would be divided among the farmers and men who had turned up. Some would end up being cooked to feed the family, others would be sold to a butcher.

Tomorrow it was back to work as usual.

I suppose the thing that as a boy I remember most about Christmas was the huge amount of food that was expected to be consumed. For many weeks, tins of chocolate fingers, toffees and bottles of boiled sweets and other rare delicacies had been collected and, as far as mother knew, were stored away in some secret corner, ready for Christmas. I wonder why she tried to keep such things hidden?

In those days there seemed to be no need to worry about when it had to be eaten by, or such things as "sell by" dates. If it looked all right, and smelled all right, then it was fit to be eaten. If everyone was feeling all right the next day, then the judgement was correct.

After the usual Christmas dinner, there always seemed to be an extra table laid with cakes, mince pies, jellies and all kinds of sweetmeats. Once this had been demolished, the table would be got ready for the late evening supper, with cold meats and pickles, cold meat pies, more mince pies and the remains of any left over poultry from the Christmas dinner. It couldn't be put in the fridge; they were not available to run on paraffin or logs. Where everyone found room to eat all that food, I never knew, but it all seemed to be eaten up pretty quickly. Very little was thrown away.

CHAPTER 16 – TIME OFF

It might appear that life was all work and very little play in those days. We did have our fair share of relaxation, maybe a little different from today, but we made the best of what was available.

Although we lived in Quethiock parish, we had more connections with the village of Tideford. I cannot recall anybody from our village entering the annual flower show at either village, maybe due to the difficulty in getting to either village. To a large number of farm workers, I suppose the shoots laid on by the Gamekeeper especially for them must have been one of the highlights of the year, judging by the numbers that came from far and wide. At the end of February or early March, was the annual pigeon shot, when one day was devoted to shooting as many wood pigeons as possible. It was the farmer's way of saving as much seed as possible. Pigeons are very fond of freshly sown seeds in the field. At the beginning of May it was time for a rook shoot, but it didn't seem quite so popular, probably because there was only a limited amount of edible flesh on a rook. Only the breasts were used. With pigeons, many a household enjoyed pigeon pie, although I cannot remember it ever being on our table.

At Callington a Dairy School was run by the County Council for the farming community, where ladies who would be employed in dairies would learn the art of making cream and butter among other dairy management skills. One day a year the school would go to an outlying village or farm to carry out demonstrations and match their skills against the locals. In 1930 the school came to Penpol, on the Quethiock road, one of the well-run County farms. Mother won Second prize for Clotted Cream, made in her old fashioned way. I was too young to remember much about it, but I can just imagine the pride she must have had with that prize.

Sports days at Tideford were well attended, and took place on the sports field opposite the Commercial Inn. There were the usual races for children and adults, plus cycle races for both groups. The school pupils were expected to do their share with dancing around the Maypole, but I recall that it didn't always work out as planned. Most boys resent being forced to dress up in funny clothes and put on shows.

The greasy pole was usually the most popular event, especially during the evening when the effects of the Simons ale served in the Commercial had time to work.

Sports days were normally a meeting of families, who lived too far apart to visit each other on a regular basis. All the family gossip was exchanged, and children were sent off to play while some of the details of events or relatives were passed from one side of the family to the other, or at least as much as they wanted to pass on.

In those days there were no such things as Parents Evenings or their equivalent where there could be discussions with the headmaster about children's schoolwork. A great deal of effort had to be put into keeping parents and Mr. Lewis as far apart as possible, especially if there were some recent incident on his mind...... and there usually was.

In 1935 the sports day at Tideford was combined with the Silver Jubilee celebrations of King George V and Queen Mary. There were extra sports and games, plus a fancy dress parade. All the school children were treated to a special tea, and we were all presented with a commemoration mug afterwards. I have still got mine.

Donald Easterbrook, a second cousin of my mother, a bit of a lad, and a well-known local wag, came over from Landrake with some of his friends for the sports and won most things. When the games were over they found some games of their own to play. They used the solitary school bell as target practice and succeeded in ringing the bell several times with stones. They cracked the bell in the process and appeared in court some time later for causing wilful damage. At the same time Donald was charged with breaking off the tops of the gate shivers at the sports field.

I think that the real highlight of the day was the fireworks and bonfire laid on at the quay during the evening. We were used to going to the quay for the bonfire on Guy Fawkes Night, but this was to be something special. For weeks all the rubbish and old wood had been turned out from odd corners in the village and surrounding area, and Len Tabb the coalman had collected it and brought it to the quay. On the last day or two a lot of tyres and old oil had appeared during the final stages of building the bonfire.

At the appointed hour the fireworks were lit at various spots around the quay with the idea of making a big spectacle of the evening. All went well until the Bonfire was lit. The first few minutes were fine, and I think everyone agreed that it was a fine sight......... until......the flames reached the tyres and the green grass and leaves that had been put in the centres. The whole Quay was enveloped in thick black smoke. We all went home with blackened faces and clothes.

Shopping trips didn't take place very often. Local shopping took place at Callington, some four and half miles away and you had to walk...... both ways. It wasn't too bad going to Callington for the first couple of miles. After crossing the River Lynher by the very narrow Medieval bridge at Clapper Bridge there was the problem of the long walk up New Down Hill, about a mile of very steep hill. Callington seemed a long way to go after that point was reached.

After our village it seemed like a large city with all the shops full of goods and electric lights everywhere. The thought of the walk home was always at the back of your mind though.

There were shops full of all the good things of life, like toys and sweets, as well as the other more mundane shops like butchers and shops selling clothes and cottons.

The only other trips out to the shops as far as I can recall were the trips to Plymouth, just before Christmas, and then only on a couple of occasions. Every boy's ambition out in the remote areas was to go to Plymouth and visit Spooner's Caves and a trip to Woolworths. We had heard all about it at school, from children who had been lucky enough to go in previous years. No other shops mattered, they were all full of food and clothes, but Woolworths was something different. It was reputed to be the experience of a lifetime, all those lights and toys, and still more toys. All you had to do was persuade somebody to let you buy some of them.

Visiting Plymouth entailed a trip to Saltash in one of those rattle-y old Western Union busses that passed through our village on three days a week. Although the busses looked large they were only about fourteen seaters, a suitable size for the narrow road to St Ive.

These busses were leftovers from those operated by the Devon Road Transport, and had been given a new coat of paint. This I understand was the only concession made towards the improved service provided. Nothing was new. The bus would take us to Saltash where the real adventure would start. The station at Saltash was part way down a very steep hill, and the busses would all meet on the level space outside the station railings.

To catch the train to Plymouth North Road usually entailed a wait, sometimes a short one, at other times a wait that seemed like hours to a boy dying to get going. The little train that would take us to Plymouth always came over the bridge from the Plymouth direction, then had to go down the Cornwall line to be turned around, before taking us back across the bridge, and then a trip in a train to Plymouth North Road Station.

That was the most exciting part of the journey, going over the River Tamar by that bridge. It looked huge, even the writing on the end was huge I. K. Brunell 1859, in gleaming white letters. There was always someone painting high up on the top tubes. They looked like little monkeys clinging to wires and girders.

If you looked down you could see the Ferry crossing from Saltash to St Budeaux loaded with cars and lorries. There were always a lot of Naval ships at anchor in the river just underneath the bridge, and further down river towards Devonport, but in those days they were just ships to us. We couldn't tell the difference between a frigate and a battleship.

The little engine at the front seemed to make hard work of getting started with a lot of steam and the occasional whistle. There was always a lot of ding….dong going on as the signalman, high up in his little box at the end of the platform, pulled levers that altered the signals for the train drivers. As Saltash Bridge only had a single track across the little local train usually had to wait for more important trains, like the Paddington to Penzance Express. These trains were pulled by giant engines, all with names in brass letters on the side, like the City of Truro. These giant monsters sometimes with about thirty carriages in tow would rattle through, in a ball of steam with huge plumes of black smoke coming out in puffs as the train gathered speed after coming off the bridge.

In those days it was every boy's dream to become an engine driver, but when an odd soot or spark came flying from one of those engines and got in you eyes and spoilt the day out, many minds were changed. Still when you think about it, a penny in the red Nestles slot machine on the platform would produce a bar of chocolate, and that could work wonders when there was soot in your eye.

The arrival at Plymouth North Road Station was a real experience as far as I was concerned. There were all those engines, of every shape and size, some shunting carriages and others shunting wagons, and some just standing around with steam coming out from various parts around the wheels.

Men with oil cans, men with red flags, and best of all were the "Wheel tappers", men with little hammers tapping the wheels to see if they were safe to go on another journey. Up and down the platforms were iron wheeled luggage trucks with full loads of boxes, baskets and suitcases, all with their destination on red and white labels. How could they possibly go astray? High up in the top of the station roof there was a one voice telling everyone where all the trains were going. If only you could hear what was being said, or even understand half of what was said.

94

All those advertising hoardings in such wonderful colours were something special. Seaside resorts looked such exciting places to go to by train. Then there were such wonderful adverts such as the Bisto twins, Cherry Blossom boot polish, cars and motorcycles, plus such ordinary things as Virol for boys and girls, and of course Oxo and Bovril.

Shell petrol had a series of very colourful posters on railway stations, and the railways themselves produced some wonderful posters of train, but I recall that Ocean Liners seemed to creep in to a lot of the more spectacular posters. Those liners were always shown as very tall and sleek, while people were always shown on the same poster as being very small.

Cigarettes were able to advertise freely in those days. A very popular advert showed a well-dressed young man standing beside a sports car stating that there was "ten minutes to wait, so mine's a minor" referring to De Reszk minor cigarettes, sold in a flat red packet with a gold band around it. Later the image was changed to that of a lady waiting, when it became fashionable for ladies to smoke. At the same time Kensitas cigarettes advertised "Four for your Friends" in a little packet of four cigarettes packed and attached to a packet of twenty cigarettes. However they didn't remind people that they had stopping giving away the silk flags that they had been putting inside their packets instead of cigarette cards. These flags were very much sought after.

The object of the trip, Spooner's Caves, was only there for the Christmas period, to attract people in to see Father Christmas. I remember that one year we went on a trip in an imaginary submarine to get to see him. Very real it was too, sitting around on seats while all kinds of fishes and items from the bottom of the sea passed by the portholes. Then there was the walk along a tunnel on the seabed to meet HIM. It all made the journey worthwhile and was so realistic that the memory is still around.

Woolworths was something quite different; a huge shop that seemed to be filled with nothing but toys at this time of the year. There was row upon row of wooden counters made up like islands, with girls and ladies rushing up and down the centre trying to serve everybody on the other side of the counters. All the customers were holding up their purchase with one hand, with money in the other, hoping to attract the attention of one of the assistants. People who accidentally dropped their money were not popular.

The counters were covered in toys of every description, some in boxes, some out loose, some inside glass divisions on the counters, but all for sale at sixpence or less. There were dolls, guns, puzzles, clockwork cars, trains, carpenter sets, books and any sort of toy you could think of and all under one roof, and all asking to be bought.

It wasn't easy to get served in large shops like Woolworths in those days, especially when you are hardly tall enough to look over the top of the counter. You had to catch the eye of an assistant that was willing to serve boys. If you made yourself noticed by knocking something over, or kept making a noise, there was at least a chance that someone would be glad to see you out of the way. Queues were a wartime invention.

Once you had made your choice of purchase and found someone to serve you, the girl would wrap it up so quickly that you wondered if you had the right toy. Once you handed over your money the girls would take it to the large shiny till in the middle of the counter and press a few buttons on the top. A bell would ring, and your hard earned money would vanish. A lot different to the wooden till at Tideford Post Office, which was considered to be quite modern, where Mr. Govett wrote something on the top and then pulled out a little drawer to put the money in. Sometimes when he got a bit flustered with so many boys in the place all at once, he would pull the drawer too far, then with luck you saw your money once more, rolling across the floor, and with a bit more luck you could get your foot on it.

We always wanted to stay in Plymouth until it got dark to see the lights, but we had to be back into Saltash early to get the only bus home.

Someone who had a day off from school to go to Plymouth just before Christmas was the hero of the class for several days, while the wonderful experience was retold with suitable embellishments many times.

During the summer months we would usually have a couple of trips out to Looe with Uncle Fred Billing, and Aunt Flo and their son Bernard, who was about my age. Uncle Fred was mother's brother and lived at Stockaton near Lundulph where they had a market garden. During the winter months we would be collected for the occasional trip to the pictures at Saltash, usually on a Saturday night.

At first they had a Model T Ford lorry converted from an open tourer car. This was later changed for a One Ton Ford market truck. Reg Number CV 66 "that had a proper gearbox". And proudly painted on the side was F. BILLING, FRUIT GROWER, LANDULPH. When we went on these trips Aunt Flo and mother used to ride in the front, and father, Ray and myself would be in the truck with Bernard. It wasn't very comfortable but it was riding.

For cinema trips the truck would be parked in the Commercial pub yard. No official car parks in those days, and the cinema was just a short walk down the road. Only black and white films and the sound wasn't too good, but they only just changed over from silent films, so we had to make allowances.

There were odd occasions when there was a problem with starting after the cinema shows. Self-starters were not fitted to all cars yet. It wasn't easy swinging that starting handle at the front, and pulling that ring with a wire attached that disappeared under the radiator to the engine. This, I found out in later years, was the choke, an essential part of starting in those days. When we did have a problem starting, a little push down the centre of Saltash Fore Street would bring it into life.

Aunt Ede, mother's sister and Uncle Vic Ruse lived at Eldridge and had a market garden. What was more important was that they had a lorry that they would sometimes come and fetch us to take us out to some function or other. Uncle Vic was a little stout man that was always full of fun and could always be relied on to start something that would end up with those boys being shouted at.

Ray and myself would sometimes go to Eldridge to stay for a few days. One good thing about going there was that they, like all the market gardeners in the district, had an old Plymouth Corporation Bus body that was used as a packing shed. Everything was brought in here to be weighed or packed for market. During the seasons it would in turn be full of flowers, or fruit so that there was always a pleasant smell about. To boys it was always warm and somewhere in the dry to play.

As all good Chapel going people, Aunt Ede and Uncle Vic were staunch Liberals. Isaac Foot was the local MP and the leading light in the local Chapels. I can well remember being at Eldridge on the lead up to the 1933 General Election, and a number of neighbours coming in to pass away an evening. We had to join in the singing of the songs that were printed on the same sort of sheets that we had for Sunday School Anniversary. They were not Hymns though, or popular songs, but rallying songs for the Liberal Party. "If you want to find our Isaac, we know where he is, right at the top of the poll" is one that I remember.

The Conservative Party had a candidate, a young man, John Rathbone, that didn't stand any chance of getting in, and that other Party was not even mentioned in Cornwall. The Labour party they called themselves. Imagine the long faces when the Conservative Party came to the top of the poll, and Isaac Foot lost his seat, never to get back to Parliament again. How could this happen? He had been a Privy Councillor too.

Just a little way down the road, mother's other brother Uncle Jack and Aunt Mary with their two sons, Fred and Clifford lived at Kingsmill Park. As if carrying on the family tradition, they were market gardeners too. Fred and Clifford were a year or two older than Ray and I, but used to come up to Eldridge to play with us, or we would go to their place, about half a mile away. They would all join in and go with us in one of the lorries for trips out to Looe, making it a real family affair, during the summer.

I remember that we had a special trip out to Looe when Uncle Vic got his new Ford one-ton lorry, R L 8918, which he kept for many years.

In those days it was usual for people who were lucky enough to own cars to tax them only from April to September. Winter motoring was not popular. Cars and lorries were taxed for either one year or three months in those days, and tax periods started on the first of January, April, July and October. At the expiry date you were given fourteen days grace to get a renewal license. If you didn't live near a Post Office that sold Vehicle Licences you had to send Money and Insurance Certificate to Truro if you lived in Cornwall.

Journeys out with Aunt Ede and Uncle Vic were usually to a Chapel gathering of some sort, but they were quite good. Social evenings were held in the barn at Smeaton Farm at least once during each winter. There was usually a good feed to support the musical and comedy items that made up the evening. The only seating was on bundles of hay and the only lighting was by hurricane lantern, so a fire was a real possibility, but we never had one. Arthur Billing (Uncle Art), mother's brother and his friend Bill Pendray were usually available to entertain in some sort of sketch I seem to remember. Bill Pendray was almost an entertainment in himself. A very tall man with pebble glasses, he always had a very bland face, and his expression would never change.

A sketch about Ten Green Bottles came up regularly, and I do remember that a wooden form with a grey cloth cover made a very good Tom Pearce's Grey Mare, to go off to Widecome Fair, and was a great hit. I seem to remember that the best bits of these evenings out was the ride home in the back of the lorry.......in the dark...and the cold.

At one stage we did have a car. There was some arrangement that we would share with Uncle Art. It was a 1919 Citroen tourer with solid disc wheels and a very high canvas roof. Not really the last word in luxury but it did give us a few trips out to see relatives.

Father started to learn to drive, but pulling on the steering wheel and shouting "Whoa" didn't have the same effect as it did on horses. I can remember going to see mother's father at his farm Tregrove Farm near Linkinhorne. It was a farm in those days, but I see that it is classified as a cottage in modern O.S. maps. That was a wonderful place, with the River Inny and Trecarrel Bridge just along the road. The bridge was only wide enough for a wagon to pass over comfortably, with granite blocks set into the sides to keep wagon wheels off the bridge sides. The river was fast running and so very clear. There was a stream running through the field beside the old farmhouse that gave a lot of pleasure to boys that didn't mind getting wet and covered in a thick clay type of mud. I got to love going to this place to stay for a few days in later years. Granfer Billing's horse Bob was his pride and joy, and he spent many a winter's night grooming him.

The Citroen car finally had a conversion carried out on it, so that it could earn its keep. The rear of the body was cut off and a small bench fitted across the rear. The drive shaft from the gearbox was disconnected and attached to the saw when in action. It could still be converted to normal for travelling on the road.

Uncle Art and his brother Uncle Eric went around cutting up wood for farmers, and eventually ended with clearing the wood at Trecarrell, just a little way down the road from Granfer Billing. Bob was brought in to help by pulling the felled trees to the saw bench.

There was no governor fitted to the engine of the little car to regulate the throttle to cope with varying thicknesses of wood, so an arrangement was made with a piece of string and a forked stick. Whoever was operating the saw bench held a knee against the fork and just pressed forward and opened the throttle when it was needed. And it worked.

While we were using the car as normal transport, we took it for a wash most Sunday mornings to the ford that crossed the old road from St Ive to Clapper Bridge, between Warren House and a little small holding with the quaint name of Enquire the Way. It is supposed to have got its name from the useful function it performed in the dark and distant past. This road was reputed to have been used by Monks travelling to help build Pillerton Church, and Pilgrims travelling to the shrines on Bodmin Moor. The Crusaders and later the Knights Templar were reputed to have used the road on their way to cross into Devon via the River Lynher at Clapper Bridge and then the Tamar.

Charles I crossed part of his army by this bridge after his victory at Lostwithiel in 1644, to meet with the main detachment in Devon.

In 1480, during the Wars of the Roses, there was conflict between Richard Edgcumb (Cotehele) and Robert Willoughby (Callington) at "Klaper Brygge" during a sever storm, and many men died. Their bodies and that of their horses were swept downstream to "Pilyton Brygge" (Pilliton Mill). Their cries and their ghosts can still be seen and heard during heavy storms and high waters. Father always swears that he saw and heard them, many years ago.

The original Clapper Bridge that gave the place its name, was swept away in the Fifteenth Century, and replaced by the bridge that now stands there.

There were very few roads in Cornwall before the mid eighteenth century, but there were numerous tracks in this area, leading to Tideford, Callington, Newton Ferrers, St Ive and Pillaton plus various farms, and few mineral mines.

A bit of a queue formed at the ford sometimes. Well, two or three market gardeners and farmers washing their light lorries. The stream was not very wide but the water was quite deep in the middle.

A medieval miniature Clapper footbridge across the ford allowed people travelling on foot to cross, but I recall that it was destroyed by an American Army lorry during the war. Although it was repaired and replaced it was never quite the same. The stone piers were replaced by bricks and mortar, while the huge stone slabs that originally formed the top were replaced by concrete.

CHAPTER 17 – ROAD REPAIRS

The arrival of the road repair gang was an exciting time for most boys during the nineteen thirties. That rattling, steaming convoy could be heard miles away, heralding its approach to one of the lay-bys normally used during the repair. The huge engine, with gleaming brass and shining paint would make its way along the roads with a lot of rattling coming from the huge front roller and the large, wide rear wheels, and the occasional whistle when the driver recognised someone, or just thought that it was time to make all the cattle get up from their resting place.

Behind the steaming monster, a tall wooden caravan would be in tow. Mounted on steel wheels it added to the noise of the procession. This caravan would be home to the engine driver if he lived too far away to travel home each evening after work. It was equipped with a bunk and a small solid fuel stove, and that was the limit of the comforts supplied by the owner. The caravan was shared as a tool store and the red glass hurricane lanterns that would be used by the night watchman. Behind the caravan would usually be found the tar covered spraying generator, again on steel wheels to add to the noise. Following this was the water carrier that was used to fill the boiler of the engine, and to supply water to assist in the laying of dust from the sand used in the repairs. One would be forgiven for thinking that the only firm that supplied these engines was R. Dingle and Sons, Stoke Climsland, whose name appeared on the boards fitted under the canopy that covered the engine, and again on the side of the caravan. All the engines that seemed to be working in this part of the country were supplied by them.

At various places in the area there were areas that were set aside for the parking of this convoy, where a supply of stone could be deposited a week or two before the repair gang arrived. One of these depots was at Tideford Cross where a large piece of wasteland had gradually been made into a hard standing with deposits of cinders from the engine and any spare stone that had not been used. There was another at Blunts in a triangular plot of ground at the top of Roosta Hill, just outside the farm gate.

A very good indication of where any road works were going to take place were the mounds of gravel, placed beside the road at regular intervals, a few days before work commenced.

A steam engine at work would draw boys from miles around to stand and wonder. It was like a magnet. If the work went on for any length of time, and you could strike up a friendship with the engine driver, you stood a good chance of some one-upmanship when you were invited to get up in the driver's area. You became very important up there with all that steam, oil and coal........until you got home and mother saw the state of your clothes.

During the thirties a lot of the roads in country areas were due for some extensive repairs, as the foundations were originally laid for the stagecoach era.

Before the First World War the Government of the day allocated huge sums of money for class 1 and 2 roads to be brought up to a "dust free" standard that motors could use. Other roads were allocated much lower sums of government cash, so were lower down the priority list. In our area, very much lower down the list.

When the foundations had been replaced, the steamroller had two large "teeth" fitted to the rear that were used to dig up the large foundation stones. These stones were used again, but not in their original state. They would be broken into stones that were not more than 2 1/2 inches diameter (this size was considered critical) by men employed as stonebreakers by the contractors. These were men who were either unemployed or were otherwise obliged to get whatever work was available. They were paid a very low wage and had to break the stones with a small hammer, whilst sat beside the road in all weathers.

During all repairs, the night watchman would put his red hurricane lanterns around to ensure that no traffic came to grief into any trenches that might be dug. In our sort of area the chances of this happening were very remote, hardly any cars passed by during the day, and at night the roads were deserted. The most likely job to take the watchman away from his brazier would be to lead a pony and trap past the steaming, clanking monster parked nearby.

A night watchman's life was pretty lonely, and the chance to talk to anyone, even an odd farm worker rolling home after an evening in the cider house of one of his mates, was some sort of relief from the boredom.

The spraying was the most usual form of repair. A fire was lit under the tar generator to heat the tar that was delivered in forty gallon barrels and lifted up by lock and chain to be poured into the generator and heated. When the tar was heated a steam pump fitted to the side of the generator would spray the tar out through a nozzle on to the road. Over the top would be thrown the gravel from the heaps beside the road, and the roller would be set to work to press the gravel into the tar. That hot tar could be smelled for miles around, and it was almost impossible to walk along a road being repaired without getting tar on your clothes or boots.

At least there were not the same problems with traffic control in those days. Arrangements could easily be made for the few regular road users, like Alf Jane's milk lorry, to be able to get through at the appointed time, with no trouble, even if it meant that work had to start an hour later than usual. There was no real rush to do anything in those days, especially in this part of Cornwall.

When I left the area in 1936 there was still one road that had not been improved in any way from the way it was in the days of the stagecoach. Bridge Road at Tideford was still made up as a stone road with sand infilling. When the weather was dry it was like walking on sandpaper, giving a grinding feeling underfoot, but when it was wet the whole road turned to a sandy mud lane at the top surface. Made wonderful splashes though.

The early 30s was a time of mixed fortune for the family as a whole. Mother's brother, Arthur, had come home from Canada a year or two before and was employed as a long distance lorry driver for Walter Glover of Kelly Bray. The vehicle he drove was a Ford Model BB articulated wagon, with a very unusual trailer body that was home-made by Mr. Glover, an engineer who could turn his hand at almost anything. On the front of the Furniture wagon body was what looked like a cross between a greenhouse and a garden shed. This was equipped with a large seat that could be used as a bed. The idea was that the owners of furniture could travel with their possessions. If the driver was travelling alone, he could use the compartment as living quarters. Uncle Art, as he was known to us, got married to Gladys Easterbrook of Newton Ferrers. She was a lovely lady from what I can remember of her. There was a wedding ceremony at Quethiock Chapel, (Blunts was not registered for weddings until 1951), and all the family from far and near came to our little house for the reception. I expect mother did all the catering. There was no one else to help out. I can vaguely remember the whole village being full of cars and lorries of every description.

After they got married Uncle Art gave up long distance driving and drove a tipper lorry for Betty and Tom of Menheniot, delivering stone from Menheniot Quarry to the Quay at St Germans for shipping to Plymouth for road building. They had a son, Ron, born in 1934. They moved from their cottage at Cutmere to a bungalow under Cadison Bury. Sadly Aunt Gladys died when Sylvia was born in 1936. Once more, mother came to the rescue and Sylvia came to live with us for a few months while things got sorted out.

Sylvia went to live with Aunt Ede and Uncle Vic at Elbridge. They had no children of their own. Ron stayed with his father and moved to a bungalow at Long Hill. Aunt Win, mother's youngest sister came to the bungalow and took care of them. That bungalow beneath Cadson Bury was dismantled, and has been rebuilt on a site on the Callington side of the river.

CHAPTER 18 – THE MOVE

Father had begun to suffer from ever increasing attacks of asthma in the early thirties, mostly due to the dust he encountered on the farm at Holwood. Although he was officially a horseman he, like everyone else, was expected to do his share at threshing and other jobs around the farm when required. On doctor's orders he was advised to find somewhere to live where the air was clear and find work without too much dust. This was mentioned to one of the hawkers that regularly visited the village with their basket of wares to sell. That basket would contain tea towels, pot scrubbers, clothes pegs and a collection of odds and ends that was always useful. At the same time, the husband of the family would buy rabbit and mole skins, that we used to tack up to dry on the inside of the linhay door.

It appeared that Mr. and Mrs. Mills as they were called had recently bought a bungalow and two fields of land, which they were going to rent out. Situated just outside Callington it sounded ideal. Eventually, after a visit to view it, it was agreed that we would take possession at Michealmas 1936.

This was all agreed before the tragedy of Aunt Gladys, so the move was convenient if nothing else, and helped to soften the blow.

It all sounded exciting to us boys, to be able to get near a town where there were reports of all sorts of things to do and see.

Although it was for his own good, Father wasn't too pleased about the move. His main concern was his animals. It took a long time for him to find homes for his cows and pigs. They were not allowed to go to market where they might fall into just anybody's hands. He had to know that they were going to be well cared for. It was with a very heart that he sent his Buttercup, the old Jersey cow that had been his favourite for many years, and old Liz the lop eared sow to go off to new homes. I spotted him many times turn away and wipe an imaginary bit of dust from his eye.

At long last the time came to say goodbye to the school and all the friends that we had made, and to the village where we had spent so many happy years. Even at eleven years old, you wonder what the future holds in a strange place, even if it was only a few miles away. It could have been the other side of the world, the little that we knew about it. There were things that would be sadly missed, like Earnest Jane's old parrot that hung outside his door during the summer, and would screech at you if you tried to speak to him. Never did get around to teaching it to swear. There was that Morris Cowley two-seater car that passed through the village at about five o'clock every evening with the driver that always waved to the children. During the summer months, when the driver's hood was folded down he would throw out old maps and odd bits of motoring literature for us. Who this phantom driver was we never did find out.

There was going to be all kinds of things to find out and get used to in a new place where we didn't know anybody or anything about the area, or what went on to keep boys amused and out of trouble.

Wonder if there would be a carpenter's shop nearby where we could go and sit if it was wet or cold and have a cup of tea with plenty of sugar in it, like Bill Jane gave us?

Would there be a little shop like the one at Tideford run by Mr. Perry, where I could collect a bundle of packets of seeds and take around the village to sell and maybe earn a few pence? There were all kinds of unanswered questions, but now the day had arrived when Hilda came over and gave us a packet of fancy biscuits and said goodbye, as we climbed into the back of Uncle Vic's lorry with the furniture and faithful old Nell.

I can remember thinking that we were a bit on the lonely side at our new house. Blunts was a small place, but here we were on our own, completely. Isolated I think you would call it. Sunnyside was a timber-framed bungalow, covered in a very heavy corrugated iron, with tongue and grooved timber interior walls. It was set in the corner of a field in Fullaford Road, about a mile from the town. There was a short drive to the back door and a little flower garden to the front with a little gate leading out to the road. It was divided from the field at the rear by a hedge and at the front by a laurel fence. The entrance to the rear drive was through a wide gate that was held shut by a chain over the granite gatepost and the end post of the gate. A gate just inside the entrance led into the 'top field' with a black timbered building. To the rear of the bungalow was a line of timber and galvanised sheds, with an earth closet at the far end.

Once more we were living without mains water and drainage and as a bonus there was no electricity, although it was available about a quarter of a mile away at Moss Side on the main road.

Mr. and Mrs. Mills, the landlords, had spent the previous six months in a tent on the driveway, but had now moved to the top corner of the field with direct access to the main Tavistock to Liskeard road at Long Hill. With their tent, of course.

They were directly involved in improving our water supply. Between them they were digging a well that was to be our only source of water for quite a few years. Mr. Mills had a deformed right foot, and it was of a convenient size to fit into a heavy gauge bucket. Into this bucket he would climb, and his wife would lower him down into the well by a windlass fixed over the top on an old lorry chassis. The bucket would be returned to the top full of the earth and shale that had been dug out, and thrown onto a heap beside the well top. They dug this well to the depth of forty-five feet by this method, before striking a source of water. It seemed to take an awful long time to dig this deep. All was not wasted though. It was a source of interest and we did learn some language that was not normally heard, especially when a bucket of spoil would accidentally hit the sides while being wound to the top and odd bits dropped on the head of George Mills. It was on a couple of occasions that Mrs. Mills put the wooden top down and left work while George was still at the bottom, but she always came back for him later.

While the well was being dug, water had to be carried from the spring in the field of Arthur Reed, who had some cattle in a field opposite. The spring was some distance away where he had built his cattle sheds near the main road.

The previous owners of our bungalow had installed a number of large covered water tanks and relied on a plentiful supply of rainwater for everyday use and for drinking.

Eventually the well was dug and a barbed wire fence was put around it to keep livestock away from the area, but no wall was ever built around the top as any form of protection for humans. There was just a wooden and galvanised trap door and the old windlass to lower down to get the water. It was always considered too dangerous for boys to get near, so getting the water to the house was always father's job.

We were still stuck with the paraffin lamps for a year or two, but these were upgraded after a while by the use of Tilley lamps. These were paraffin lamps, but were pressure fed by a small pump in the base, after lighting a methylated spirit wick that heated a vaporiser, which in turn ignited a mantle. It gave off a very bright light compared to the old type lamps, but the loud hissing noise was a bit of a nuisance. After a few more years we went all modern and had Calor Gas lighting in most of the rooms. Occasionally we ran out of gas cylinders if Mr. Tucker from Coads Green hadn't arrived with refills on time, but we were usually well supplied.

As the bungalow had been built on a slight slope there were three or four steps from the front door down to garden level. Around these four steps had been built an oversized glass front porch. As it was fully enclosed it was more like a greenhouse.

In this greenhouse or front porch as mother insisted on calling it, mother would keep all her precious plants. Cuttings would be taken from here and there and everywhere, and rooted in the warmth of the sun. No problems about which compost to use. Everything was rooted in ordinary garden soil, and the amazing thing was that it all grew. When it came around to winter, all she did was put a few newspapers over the top of her plants and they would come back in the spring, without being affected by frost. She would give friends and relatives cuttings from plants with the assurance that they were easy to grow, but they didn't meet with the same level of success.

The whole idea of the move to Callington was firstly father's health, and secondly to try to build a better life for the whole family. Being a farm worker in those days was not the most glamorous job, and the prospects of any better way of life were nil. The idea was that we would keep a few pigs and poultry, and the lower field would be used as a market garden, where the produce could be sold to local shops or sent to market. When we moved in we had empty fields, a few fowls that we had brought from Blunts, not very much money and a whole lot of hope. We had to start from scratch. Before we could have any livestock we had to build a pig's house to keep them in. We started with a "sectional" fowls house, in other words a fowls house that came in pieces and you put it together yourself..... Very modern in 1936.

Father built a galvanised pigs house and then we bought a couple of pigs. At odd times plots of ground were cleared by hand to get something growing in the ground that would produce some sort of income as soon as possible. Life for anyone who earned their living from the land in those days was very hard but when the only mail that came were bills, and there was no money coming in, life was that much harder. Father would work from first light in the morning until dark. There was always something that he could find to do. In the early days I think we thought that we were worst off in every way than when we lived at Blunts, but a couple of good summers, and a lot of hard work soon began to make it all worthwhile. Sunnyside lived up to its name and was a wonderful spot to be when the sun shone.

Eventually Aunt Ede and Uncle Vic legally adopted Sylvia, but we still had a number of visits, so that we didn't loose touch. Secretly I think Mother was longing to have Sylvia to bring up as a sister for us boys.

She would then have someone to make pretty dresses and ribbons and bows for. There was always room for one more in our house. As things turned out, mother had her work cut out with the new house and fields, and the work it entailed.

CHAPTER 19 – NEW SCHOOL, NEW TOWN

Schools were something that we had to face very shortly after moving into the new house. Hardly had time to get to know anybody before going off to Callington to look for the Junior School for Ray and the Senior School for me. My new school looked massive compared to the tiny Tideford School. There was one advantage that seemed to be a very good idea. The headmaster, Mr. Sam Rickard didn't believe in the cane. Apart from this most welcome change to the normal routine of school life, it appeared to be a very conventional school. Among the other welcome items was the news that every year there was a school trip to somewhere that, to children of our age, was only a name on the map. Something to look forward to though.

Although there was no cane used in the school, there were other forms of punishment that were much worst. Keeping a fellow in for an hour when the sun was shining and everyone else was outside was terrible. Much better to get the punishment over in a few short strokes.

One teacher was Mr. Ronald Johns, who loved cricket, and played for the Callington First Eleven. He was in charge of the sports, that all boys had to do on one half day each week. That meant cricket during the summer months, even if it did bore you to tears. What he will be remembered by, for most people who had the somewhat doubtful privilege of being taught by him, was his aim. No matter what he was doing, or what he had in his hand at the moment of being noticed doing something other than he intended, he would throw it. His aim was most deadly accurate, and some of the things that he threw would land very heavy.

The thing that I hated most was that school uniform, especially those stupid hats. The cap was a little round thing that didn't seem to want to stay in place under any circumstances, and was always getting lost. And the thing that boys hated, ties. At Tideford we wore what we wanted, but here it had to be uniform all the time. We had never been brought up with such things. Ties, blazers and shoes were not the thing for country boys. And then there was that terrible thing....homework. Not a bit like Tideford.

It must be admitted though that there were some improvements over Tideford School. The Senior School was only a few years old, so it was quite modern for the times. Hot and cold water with washbasins in all the toilets, and toilets that were clean and warm, without being awash with water smelling of Jeyes Fluid. No more Tortoise stoves giving off coke gasses, but central heating with hot water pipes and huge radiators in all the classrooms.

Pasties could be placed on hot water pipes if the outside papers were marked with the owner's name, but were not allowed in the classrooms, only in the cloak rooms. There was the occasional prank played on certain pasties but not very often. The most usual thing to do was to move the precious paper bag containing the pasty to another position from where it had been placed. That caused confusion.

The school bell rang as usual, but there never seemed to be so many late arrivals, perhaps it was because most pupils lived within a short distance of the school. Anyone who was late seemed to call it a day and take the whole day off, rather than stay behind late for two or three evenings as punishment. It was much less trouble, and there seemed to be little chance of anyone checking why you were absent.

Some things didn't seem to change though. We were all expected to leave the school premises during the dinner break, and find something else to do, or someone else to annoy. As usually, mother usually had a few little shops for us to visit, to collect items or order something. One shop that we always seem to be visiting was the Co-op in Callington Fore Street. Before it was modernised the Plymouth Cooperative Society as it was known consisted of a fairly large shop with an entrance door on either side of a large central plate glass window. Inside there was a large mahogany counter that ran along two sides of the shop with a separate counter for cheese and bacon on the other side. Leaning against the front of the counter were opened bags of rice, dried fruit and all kinds of produce, to be weighed out as customers asked for it. Very little was pre-packed and most of what was had been packed in the shop during quiet spells.

When we had to go into this shop to buy anything, we had to give the Co-op share number for every purchase. Instead of a discount every regular customer was allocated a share number, which was recorded on every receipt, a copy of which went off to headquarters in Plymouth. At the end of the year you would be told how much your discount plus a bit of interest was worth, and where and when it could be collected. "Divi days", as they were known, were always looked forward to. And how the

"Divi" was spent was usually the subject of much planning for most families, to buy something special. That share number was important but it could easily be forgotten among the other things that had to be remembered in a schoolboy's head. Although it was often forgotten in 1936, I know it now that it is fifty years out of date. 2890 is firmly embedded in my mind.

In those days all the Co-op customers who lived outside the town had their groceries delivered once a week. The Co-op parcel came all wrapped up in stout brown paper, and tied up with a strong piece of string. The parcel was delivered by the bread delivery van that passed the lovely hot bread smell to the paper-covered parcel. The bread man was responsible for collecting the payment for the parcel and for any sale of bread and cakes that he might make. He used to give out a little receipt, not much larger than a postage stamp, with carbon on the back, which was supposed to be kept, "in case of dispute" it said at the bottom. Most people threw them away within a few minutes of receiving them, or else do as my mother did, put them in a convenient spot until there was no chance of a mistake being made by anyone, then threw them away.

I used to watch those parcels being made up in the shop sometimes. It was a work of art. Butter, cheese, bags of sugar and flour, plus tins and packets of all shapes were gathered together by the shop assistant, and placed on a large sheet of brown paper. The goods would be moved and placed in position so quickly that it looked as if they were meant to slot together. A few quick folds of the paper and a few twists of the cord and the string would be holding it all together, the knot had been tied and the string would be arranged to cut itself at the end of the operation, all within a few seconds. Freda Coombes' fingers moved so fast that it was impossible to see how she did it.

The shop on the corner at the top Back Lane was run by the Attwood family, and they had a much better idea for discount. Depending how much was spent, you got a metal disc representing coins with your change. When you had saved enough, they could be spent, just like money, in their shop of course. No numbers to remember, so less trouble for boys who managed to forget, with the added bonus that it might be possible to keep the discs and spend them on some sweets at a later date. On occasions other shops had to be visited to carry odd items home. I suppose the most visited shop must have been Buckingham's, the leather shop, to buy hob-nails for working boots, or toe protectors and heel "Scoots" for boys boots and shoes. Cards of Bilkeys toe protectors were sold, with eight metal pads of various shapes, fitted with three very short nails built into them. One kick at a stone and they would come off. More trouble.

Mr. Buckingham sold everything made of leather, or anything connected with leather. Nails, springs, leather and rubber soles were all in the shop somewhere. Every inch of the walls was covered with stock, from horsewhips to saddles. Small, but a bit on the stout side, Mr. Buckingham spoke with a bit of a lisp, and was the subject of a lot of imitation and hilarity. To most children of the town, and to a lot of adults too, he was often referred to as Billy Blass Spligs.

Mr. Millman was the corn merchant at the top of Back Lane, opposite the blacksmith shop. We were sent to get a small bag of maize for the fowls if the delivery of corn was in any way delayed, or father had been a bit too generous and we ran short. I can remember that Mr. Millman didn't like weighing out fourteen pounds of maize. He couldn't see why we couldn't take home a full one hundredweight (112 pounds). At the end of a mile even fourteen pounds were heavy enough.

There were many differences between our old and new homes, but some things didn't change very much. House martins still made their mud nests under the eves of houses, but there were more of them, houses and birds. Some telegraph poles had about a dozen wires stretching from one post to the next to accommodate all the birds before migration, where we had only been used to seeing about two wires at most. There was a difference in the noise they made too. Girls still screamed when they were confronted by a lizard in a Swan Vestas box, with only their front legs outside, to crawl along a school desk or similar.

For the first time for many years mother could get to the shops when she wanted anything urgently, and that relieved us boys of a lot of shopping and gave her a chance to meet new people. The town of Callington was only a small market town with a population of around 5000, but it did seem to have a good variety of shops. Ironmongers were among the most important to boys, they sold bikes and the bits to repair them.

Doney and Hancock had a shop at West End. The front was only small, just two smallish shop windows with a door between, but it did go back a long way. The floor I remember was wooden, and seemed to wave up and down, to give some sort of level to varying odd rooms that had been added at different times. As people walked on the floor that somehow resembled a footpath through the shop, the footsteps made a hollow sound. Along the full length of the shop was a wooden topped mahogany counter, and every few yards was attached a brass ruler, three foot long. Curtain wires, webbing, wooden dowels, electrical wire, and anything else that needed to be sold by length were measured out on these rules. Behind the counter were, what must have amounted to, hundreds of drawers, holding every small item anyone could possibly imagine. Except of course the item you needed.

The rest of the shop was full of items for the home, garden and farm. From lino for the kitchen floor to a hoe for the garden, pots, pans and fertilizers were all there somewhere. The cycle section was a bit disappointing, just a few tyres and tubes and usually about three bikes, all expensive models.

Mr. Doney was a small man who spent his time behind the counter of the shop, and was just like any other member of the staff. Mr. Hancock was a slim balding man, who spent most of his time out of town visiting old and new customers. He called on most farms and smallholdings once a month to collect monies owed, if any, and to collect orders for goods to be delivered. Within a day or two the brown painted Bedford lorry would deliver sheets of galvanize, or metal pig's troughs to the door.

Biscombes had a much larger ironmongery shop in Fore Street, with (for the times) a much more modern lay out inside. Small counters were half hidden away at various places, to try to give the impression that the goods on offer were more important than getting the money in the till. But the goods were all around you with a price ticket attached, the same as all the other shops. Again, everything for house and farm was on offer, even furniture in a separate shop near the Market Gate. As well as the general ironmongery sales, they employed two blacksmiths to repair farm implements and general smithy work. Beside the blacksmith shop at the rear of the main shop were tinsmiths and an assortment of small workshops.

All over East Cornwall could be seen windmills for pumping water, with a tail that proclaimed to all the world that it was installed by Biscombes of Callington.

Biscombes did keep a few more cycles than Doney and Hancocks, and more spares. At one stage they set up a complete cycle department but it didn't last long. Boys like to look, ask questions and dream, not buy.

Trewartha, Gregory and Doidge were a more recent firm, which had been formed by three ex employees of both of the other ironmongers. They had premises in Church Street that led right through to Well Street. They also had a monthly visit to most of the farms in the area, and were becoming well established in the area when we went to Callington to live. And they had a good bicycle section.

The town boasted six butchers to feed the hungry. Not many vegetarians around in those days. Roseveares were in Saltash Road, Parrott in Fore Street, Bonds at West End, Rickard in Church Street, Edwards in Well Street and Hooper in Back Lane. Butcher Edwards delivered to our house once a week in his old Morris Cowley converted car. It was originally a saloon with a door at the rear, designed to allow children in and out without opening doors to the other street traffic. Butcher Edwards had a series of varnished removable plywood panels that could dive the rear section of the car from the front, after removing the seats, and allowed him to use it as a van. For private use, just remove the panels, and replace the seats. Never mind the smell of meat.

The rest of the town was made up of all the various shops and trades that keep a small community fed and clothed.

The main hairdresser for ladies and gents was near the Tavistock Road end of Fore Street. It was run by a Mr. Squance who rode a motorbike and sidecar in from Harrowbarrow every day. He would give old George Hawk, a local character, a ride into town on occasions. One day the bike stopped outside our gate, and the cause of the stoppage was diagnosed as being because the spark plug had worked loose and been blown out of the engine. After a while spent searching for the lost plug George Hawk said, "let's not bother about a little old thing like that, let's get on".

Mother's youngest brother Cecil had tuberculosis in his leg when he was a boy and had to wear a high boot. He had served an apprenticeship with Mr. Squance as a hairdresser, and had moved on to open up his own shop at Gunnislake.

Tuesdays the whole of Fore Street had a clean down. If possible, pavements were scrubbed and all little corners were cleared of rubbish, ready for the big day on Wednesday. All the windows of shops were filled with the goods on offer, and before leaving work all the shops had wares that normally stood outside, all ready for the next day's trading. Wednesday was Market Day, and the whole area seemed to come into town, either to buy, sell, shop or just look. From early morning, cattle would start to arrive in the Cattle Market in Saltash Road, some in Glover and Uglows modern cattle lorries, others on foot from farms from all over the district. Young calves would be brought to market in carts, with the mother cow walking behind, making reassuring noises to her offspring.

What a mess they used to make on the road, and it was not exactly sweet smelling either. Pigs and poultry would arrive in farm carts, vans or trailers, all to be divided up and penned in convenient lots for sale by auction. At ten o'clock, cattle were brought into the main ring to be sold by an auctioneer, who seemed to be talking in a language that very few people could understand. There seemed to be a lot of waving of sticks and strange movements by the farmers stood around the ring, until eventually the auctioneer would slap his clip board with his stick and the animal that had been the centre of attraction would be taken out of the ring and replaced by another. How anybody ever knew who had bought what and for how much was very difficult to work out, but the farmers seemed to know.

Pigs and sheep were held in pens that stretched the length of the market, with a galvanized roof to offer some protection from the elements. There was a wooden walkway about a foot wide fitted to the top of the centre of the pens where the auctioneer, with his assistants would stand and take bids. Again they spoke so fast and in such a strange language that I could never really follow what was gong on.

While all this was going on in the Cattle Market, butter, cream, eggs, fruit and vegetables were being sold in the Pannier Market at a much more sedate pace, usually by farmer's wives. The Market Manager, Mr. Jago would issue a stall number to each would-be stallholder, and that was the stall you would occupy. There was no favouritism, so that some people, by coming early would get a favourable position.

The town shops were always busy on market days with all the farmer's wives and families coming to do their shopping. If a good price had been fetched for anything that was sold in the market, then this was a golden opportunity to spend a bit extra.

Later afternoon, and the whole town would empty. Some cattle would be driven to new homes or even back to their original homes if the required price had not been reached. One way or another the market would be emptied, and all the pens scrubbed down, ready for the next sale.

Not all the farmers went home at the end of the day. The Bulls Head, the Coachmakers Arms, the Commercial, and the Blue Cap had been open from ten o clock, and some farmers had made some good sales in the market. Others were drowning their sorrows over the poor sales they had made, or maybe had not made. In the courtyard behind all the establishments, or in some other convenient spot, there would be a pony and trap, or a pony and jingle. All that was needed was a friend to load the farmer into the driving seat and give the pony a hearty slap. They knew the way home. Others were not so fortunate, they had to walk, or at least try to. One or two from outside town would take a few hours to travel the odd mile, allowing for a little sleep along the way.

Market day gave some of the older boys a chance to earn a bit of ready cash, doing a bit of cattle driving for someone they knew, maybe getting an afternoon off school at the same time. Unofficial of course.

Throughout the year there were various special markets, for various grades of cattle, but to the majority of people in the area, the October market with the Honey Fair was the most important.

In the Saltash Road recreation field would come all the fun of the fair, supplied by Whitelegg and Sons or Anderton Rowlands. Behind beautiful gleaming steam engines would come the dodgems and various roundabouts that would attract people from a wide area to come and spend money and have a few hours of relaxation.

The field would be filled with the massive steam engines and special Showman's type lorries, towing the huge caravans used by the more senior Showmen. These caravans were an attraction admired by all, proudly displaying their elaborate mirrors and sparkling crystal glasses that were on display through elaborately engraved windows. Strategically placed soft light showed the magnificent interiors of these luxury caravans off to advantage.

To schoolboys, Honey Fair by night was like something from another world. What a wonderful sight. Those steam traction engines that had drawn those exciting rides into town, were now displayed in all their glory brightly lit by dozens of coloured bulbs, as they went about their work of driving generators to light the rest of the fairground. So quietly, just the odd hiss of steam, and that brightly coloured revolving flywheel to let the world know that it was still working. The brass work would be glittering, and the paintwork shining and that huge flywheel turning over so silently with the various colours merging into a kaleidoscope of moving colour.

The huge Noah's Ark roundabout had its own steam engine fitted in the centre, to drive the wooden animal rides around the track. It was a showpiece in its own right, and the steam-powered organ fitted in beside it was loud enough to make any other type of music surplus to requirements. Many people would spend the whole evening just listening to the organ music. It was so good.

There were lorries and vans to tow light caravans and some of the lighter loads, but the huge Showman's engines were the stars of the show. The fun fair was usually in full swing for at least three days and nights. During the days, running repairs would be carried out, and I used to watch with more than a passing interest how those brilliant pictures got painted on the various roundabouts and facia boards. Although it looked so easy to get four colours of paint on a one-inch paintbrush and get it to flow exactly where needed, it was much easier said than done.

Between the main showground attractions of roundabouts and dodgem cars, were all the small sideshows that seemed to gobble up all the odd pence from your pocket at an alarming rate. And it all looked so easy to win. When, on the odd occasion you did win, the prize never seemed to have the same amount of glitter and glamour that it had when it was on the shelf, waiting to be won. Rifle ranges, darts, and candyfloss, all found a small corner, along with the fortune-tellers, strong men acts and bearded ladies. There was usually a Boxing Booth, where young men would try their luck against the resident boxers who would challenge all comers to last three rounds for a £5 prize, forgetting to mention the referee had his favourite boxers. For the more genteel, there were always the Flea Circus, Fish and Chip vans and Toffee Apple stalls.

On the Saturday night, all the young men and girls would dress up and have fun. On the Sunday, in a few short hours, the whole lot would be packed and moved on to the next town, usually to Tavistock for the Goose Fair.

Callington would once more become its quiet peaceful self. Landlords of the various hostelries would replenish their stocks, Underhills the Chemist would sell a record number of headache pills, and some people, like George Hawk from Harrowbarrow, would go home for the first time for many days and nights. The rest of the town would be counting the financial cost of a few days and nights of fun, wondering if it was all worth the expense.

CHAPTER 20 – JOINING IN

The town didn't boast a Railway Station, although at the turn of the century, plans had been drawn up to run a line from Saltash, but it had not arrived in the late thirties. Mustn't rush these things. There was a station at Kelly Bray, which had adopted the name of Callington. This was a little single-track line from Bere Alston, calling at Calstock, Gunnislake, Luckett and Latchley. Originally laid to transport minerals from the large numbers of mines in the area it had been adapted to carry passengers, and had retained this role when all the mines closed down at the turn of the century. If all else failed there was always a joke to tell about the Kelly Bray Express.

When we moved to Callington it was much easier to have a day out in Plymouth, without the problem of catching the one and only bus home. Busses were a little more frequent and there were late busses. We didn't venture out very often, but when we did we would have a full day out with dinner, usually in Sellick's Restaurant, I believe in Ebrington Street. Not that it was very posh, despite the name, but it was good food and cheap. There were roast meats for grown ups, but most children ended up with a pasty…as usual. That way there were no problems with gravy getting on best ties or suits.

My first school trip was to Aldershot to see the Military Tattoo. A ride on the train to Bere Alston was the first part of the journey, to join the main body of schoolchildren on the larger train. The trip to Aldershot was uneventful as far as I can recall, and so was the rest of the day. That evening we all got to the area where the Tattoo was to take place, with what seemed hours to spare. I was introduced to what was then advertised as the "finest ice cream" available. I bought an almost solid block of almost pure white Walls Ice Cream. To me it was a tasteless lump of something disgusting. Not a bit like the ice cream from Johno, or even Mr. Cox on the corner of Fore Street and Saltash Road. The only part of that trip that I enjoyed was the trip home in the dark. Rushing through the night at some terrific speed, the huge engine at the front was pushing out steam and smoke that seemed to be coming back over the carriages like some fast moving cloud. The glow from the firebox was reflected under the smoke, making it look as if the whole engine was on fire. I tried to paint that scene many times, but could never get anything to look remotely like it. Another talent that didn't meet with success.

To earn a bit of cash, I took a job on Saturday mornings, delivering fruit and vegetables for Ralph Deacon, who ran a small shop in Liskeard Road. First, I had to go out and call on customers and get their order, then go out again when the order had been made up. Everything was done on my old bike that at one time belonged to mother. With a box wired on to the handlebars there was no guarantee that the rod brakes would work and there was the odd mishap when apples, turnips and myself would end up on the street. Still the money was good, sixpence (2 1/2 p) for a morning's work and the same again if I took a basket of fruit to the cricket field on fine Saturday afternoons. I hate the game and found it boring, but a small adjustment to the retail price of pears being sold to the visiting spectators can work wonders to relieve boredom.

I never was particularly fond of hanging around the town during the days, with nothing much to do. I didn't mind my own company to be free to get out in the fields or over the moors. There was always something to see that you didn't know what it was and then the satisfaction of find out from books when you got home.

With less time walking to and from school then at Blunts, there was more time to explore the country around our new home. Sunnyside was in an area known as Silver Valley, but why this name I never did find out. Although there was a large number of disused mines that at one time produced tin and minerals of every description, silver was not one of them. However this did not stop the boys of the area from digging over the spoil heaps to see if anybody had missed anything years ago. In defence of the name though, it is shown on the first Ordinance Survey Map as the location for a Silver Mine. So perhaps there was a hidden reason for its name.

Many happy hours were passed away in those old mine workings. The disused engine house of the East Cornwall mine was home to birds of every description, which made their nests among the ivy that climbed to the top of the crumbling walls. You were often aware of a pair of owl's eyes keeping a watchful check on all that was going on. There was danger from old mine shafts, but what is life without a bit of danger when you are young. There was a hidden entrance to a tunnel that was intended to connect with another tunnel coming from Kit Hill, but the connection was never made. The section of tunnel at Fullaford was probably not more than one hundred feet into the hillside, but the darkness made it very scary. A colony of bats inhabited the tunnel and added to the excitement when they flew around your ears. Just the place to show off your bravery to school friends who came out from the town. Alas, the tunnel was sealed off around 1938 on orders from the mine owners in the interest of safety.

The old workings were a safe and waterproof haven for a lot of "gentlemen of the road" who would find shelter here at the end of the day. It was the halfway stop between the institution at Tavistock and the one at Liskeard. At both places they would get a bed for the night and a meal. Silver Valley was a day's walk from each, so very convenient. Water was available in a little stream and there were plenty of rabbits around if they felt like "one for the pot".

Our bungalow lay between the main road from Tavistock and this free lodging house. We did get a lot of these gentlemen and sometimes, lady travellers calling at the door, looking for free food, or a shilling for a cup of tea. I don't know where they were going to buy that cup of tea. This all came to an end when Nell our little terrier saw them. She would let them come inside the large outside gate and let it close behind them. Once inside the gate then Nell would strike. With a closed gate behind them, and no way out except to open the gate which meant walking backwards or turn away from the dog......panic stations. Nell was no fool. Not that she would bite anyone, but no one was willing to take the risk. The sight of those bare teeth would put doubts in anyone's mind. It is always said that tramps leave secret signs outside houses where there are dogs, and I think it must be true. After the first few months we never had any more callers. The coalman was perfectly safe, as long as he didn't come inside the gate with a sack on his back. With a sack of coal on his back, Nell would hold him by the trouser leg until she was told that it was alright to let him in. The postman was fair game too, and always stood outside the gate and shouted "Where's the dog, missus". When Nell died Whisky, one of her sons took over guard duties, and made a very good job of it. He had been well briefed by his mother.

There was never any shortage of interesting places to explore. A walk along the little lane at the bottom of Arthur Reeds field would bring you out, after a lot of mud, to tiny Dupath Well Chapel. This was a fourteenth century Baptismal Church made of granite blocks, with an immersion well occupying almost half of the floor space. The stories that were connected to this place would scare off most of the children from the district, so it was normally deserted. Being at the bottom of a farmyard didn't encourage many people to visit it.

Through the farmyard and a little further up the road there was an extension to the lane that was very rarely used. Brambles grew across the path, and stinging nettles and young trees made it quite an obstacle course. At the top was a little quarry with stone that had an unusual look about it. The lower half of the quarry was filled with water, it was even reputed to be bottomless guarded by a whirlpool, and with some strange monster guarder the lower water inlet. I knew this was not true. Mark Orchards Labrador, "Keeper", swam across the lake many times to prove it.

The Boy Scouts at this time were run by a W. H. Paynter, a local historian who would organise cycle trips out to some place of interest, such as The Cheesewring and the Hurlers. He seemed to have much more information about these places than any book could tell you. That stone that looked different was the Balston Down axe factory, where stone-age men made and bartered battle and domestic axes. When I was told that some axe heads were still to be found among the spoil heaps, I went in search. One was found but in poor condition, but Mark Orchard found some that were in super condition. Across the road we were taken to the site of a prehistoric henge that very few people seemed to know about. Like a miniature Stonehenge it was made of wooden pillars. The pillars are long since gone, but the earth mound is still visible.

A lady who was very well informed on local history was Mrs. Eva Foot, the wife of Isaac Foot, one time Liberal MP for the area. They had made their home at Pencreber, a fine eighteenth century house at the top of Newbridge Hill, a mile outside the town. Mrs. Foot was the grand daughter of one of the leading Methodists in Cornwall, and had strong connections with West End Chapel. I knew her best as my Sunday School teacher at West End Sunday School. A rather short lady she was a very popular figure around the town. Boys of twelve years old were not the easiest pupils to have in a class, but she had no problems. With having sons of her own, she had probably met most of the problems at some time in the past. Michael Foot, MP and one time Labour Party Leader, and Lord Caradon were just two of her sons. I think that the thing I will always remember Mrs. Foot for is that every Sunday she always spoke to each of her pupils as an individual and listened to all you had to say, and if you had a problem she would try to resolve it. A very fine lady who will long be remembered with affection by everyone who knew her.

At home the stock of pigs and poultry was increasing. New poultry houses had been built, and a large piggery built at the bottom of the "top field". The "Lower field" was fully tilled and producing cash crops. During the spring, flowers were picked from the thousands of bulbs that had been planted, bunched, boxed and sent off to Covent Garden every day. There were buckets of flowers either waiting to be bunched or waiting to be packed into special boxes in every corner of the outhouses and indoors as well. Bill Burze, a near neighbour, would collect the boxes every morning in his little lorry, converted from an Austin taxi and take them to Callington. He would deliver them, along with his own boxes to Mrs. Brimblecombe's pasty chop and Café. She had a small Western National Bus office at one end, where parcels to and from Saltash Station were collected and delivered. The bus to Saltash had more space taken up by boxes of flowers than by passengers, and the Western National Bus Company made a fortune.

From Saltash Station the flowers would go by rail to Covent Garden. Anemones, potatoes, cabbages, turnips, peas and beans filled the rest of the fields at various times of the year, although strawberries dominated the summer crops.

CHAPTER 21 – DARK DAYS AHEAD

During the summer months all hands would be recruited to pick strawberries that were planted in more than half of the field. This was a backbreaking job, and when the sun was shining in the middle of the day, a back burning job as well. After picking, all the fruit had to be packed into punnets or two pound chip baskets. During the season, a constant flow of fruit wholesalers and shopkeepers from seaside resorts came to buy the fruit. They travelled many miles, from Port Isaac, Newquay, Bodmin and St Austel, to be able to put fresh Cornish strawberries on their tables, with Cornish Clotted Cream of course. The local shops and private customers came as well, but there was usually enough to go around, whenever they came. Fruit was being picked almost continuously from first light until dusk. Everywhere you went there was the smell of strawberries, and every available inch of space had baskets of the ripe sweet smelling fruit, waiting to be moved on.

For myself, the choice of career had to be faced. At the age of fourteen, we were expected to leave school and start to earn a living. Not only was it expected, the schools didn't want to see you, there were others needing your place. The choice of jobs was limited for school leavers, even in those days. Callington had no industries, only small shops and small businesses. Travel outside the town was very difficult with limited busses and trains. It was not normally a case of what you would like to do with your life, but what was available. Most people opted for a compromise job, and changed at the first opportunity. Fortunately I knew what I wanted to do, but the vacancies were few and far between.

Glover and Uglows garage at Kelly Bray was my first choice of employment, but there were no vacancies.

I was sent to look for my own job, so with best suit and a lot of hope I travelled around all the garages in the area. Eventually I arrived back at the nearest garage to home, Pengelly Garage at Moss Side, owned by Mr. Harrott. Situated just a few hundred yards up the road it was not ideal, too small really, but it was a job. There was a little problem though.

The job was for a four-year apprenticeship but a premium of twenty pounds had to be paid before I could start. However mother and father agreed and I was eventually signed up to serve for four years. At long last I was going to be in the money, a wage at the end of every week. What you could do when you are a wage earner, and all the things you could buy. That was a short-lived dream. The wages were 2s 6d (12 1/2 p) a week for the first year, and a whole 5/- (25p) for the second, 7/6 (36p) for the third, and a whole 10/- (50p) for the final year. However I left school and started on my two-month probation period in 1939.

While we lived at Blunts we didn't really realise how far behind the rest of the world we were as far as cars were concerned. Only occasionally were modern cars seen, when we had a trip into Plymouth, and then, as boys we were under the impression that they were almost confined to the cities. I don't think that we realised that just a few miles away, even at Callington, people were buying and running modern cars.

It appeared that most of the old cars around were either in or heading for George Orchards scrap yard on Long Hill. At Blunts we were two and a half miles from a petrol pump, but here there were petrol pumps everywhere. On the roadside at St Anne's Chapel on the Tavistock Road there were two stations just set up on the roadside bank. No old nonsense about fire and explosion regulations. Storage tanks were laid, fully exposed in an enlarged roadside ditch, and a wooden platform with pumps attached placed over them, from which petrol was served. As the pumps were hand operated, electricity was not essential. After dark the pump owners just didn't come out of their house to serve. It was very much like some of the old movies.

Blunts is still two and a half miles from the nearest petrol pump today (in 1992).

At Pengelly Garage we were very modern with electricity to drive the pumps, all except one. Although there was mains electricity available for the few houses, the garage had its own generator for its own use and for charging wireless accumulators and car batteries. An apprentice was a little different from years later. In 1939 you started by doing all the odd jobs and learnt your trade by joining in with the work and watching how jobs were carried out. If you needed any technical details you borrowed books and read about it, if you could find someone that had such a book. No such things as Technical College or Day Release. No good going to the library, they only kept books that people would enjoy reading.

It became one of my duties to serve petrol when anyone came to the forecourt. The most popular brand was Dominion at 1s 4 1/2 d (7p) approx a gallon. Next popular was shell at 1/8d a gallon (7 1/2 p). National Benzol at 1s 7 ½ d was next but the most expensive, and the very best was Esso Ethyl, for high performance cars at 1/8d a gallon.

The Esso pump was the one hand operated pump, and the one that I had the most trouble with. To deliver petrol the nozzle was placed in the tank of the car as usual, and then the fun began. High up on the rear of the pump a lever had to be moved to show how many gallons were required. A long lever hung down between two glass bottles at the top of the pump. This lever had to be worked to and fro and one of the glass bottles would fill up with petrol. Each glass held half a gallon. When the glass was filled, another lever with a slide that connected both bottles had to be given a sharp push towards the empty glass and start pumping all over again, while the first glass was draining into the car tank. The problem was that the sharp push that the instructions stipulated was more than just hard. Not being very tall the lever was above my head, which didn't help things. Wonder why everybody who needed Esso Ethyl always bought petrol in such large quantities, instead of the odd gallon as other customers for the less petrol required. The National Benzol pump caused some minor problems but they could be overcome. To keep all the pumps on the same level, the Benzol pump was built on a high plinth, so I had to climb up on the plinth to get the nozzle out of the pump before delivery and again after serving.

Looking back, it is surprising how much the motorcar changed in a few short years during the mid 1930s. By 1936 wheels became smaller and wider, car bodies had lost that square box look, and engines became much quieter. The starting handle had been replaced by a self-starter, and on some cars, when the brakes were applied there was a reasonable chance of the car stopping. By 1939 there were some very stylish and luxurious cars available. The ignition switch had been replaced by an ignition key, in many cases only a very primitive flat key, but a step in the right direction. Some cars were even fitted with door locks. There was no need to lock cars in those days. Car theft was not yet a part of life. Although there were a few places in Plymouth where you pay to leave your car while shopping, it was at private garages and public houses, although parking places for bicycles were in every town and city, where you left your bike and it was stored, cleaned and oiled for 6d.

Car parks as we know them today did not exist. If you went shopping you just drove to the shop door and stopped. No need to lock the car, it would still be there when you returned, and anything left inside would be quite safe. Sounds like Utopia.

Mr. Harrott ran an old car for his hire car work. It was a Wolseley 21/60, of 1932 vintage, Reg Number OD 8993, in beautiful condition. A very impressive car, with a large spare wheel set into each front wing. It was my job to keep this monster clean and polished, and to clean those terrible wire wheels.

During my two-month trial period, I didn't get very involved with the mechanical work in the garage. A few punctures came my way for repair, and I was taught all about the petrol pumps and what oil to supply for different cars. Oh…and how to swear when things went wrong.

At fourteen years of age there were much more important things to do than try to keep up with world affairs on the wireless. I remembered Mr. Chamberlain coming home from Germany, and telling everyone about "peace in our time", so we had nothing to worry about. Then just as I was ending my trial period, father started to seem a bit worried, and talking about what was going on in the world after every news broadcast. Then on a Sunday morning he called me in to listen to the wireless, saying that I ought to listen, because it might be important. He had never done this before. I can remember those words now. "We are at War with Germany". Father went very quiet, then looked to me and said "Perhaps it won't last very long". Father didn't normally say very much in a serious way, to Ray or myself, only just talk to us in normal conversation. I didn't really know what he meant by that remark. That Sunday afternoon when I went into the town there were little groups of men in their Sunday best suits, all strangely quiet.

By this time two uncles, Arthur and Eric, were the proud owners of an old Fordson Tractor with steel wheels and were earning a living carrying out ploughing and other contract work for other farmers in the area. To travel from one farm to the next entailed fitting steel bands over the spike like lugs of the rear wheels to avoid damaging the roads.

The front wheels had a very narrow centre point to the rim that left a white mark on the road. Pneumatic tyres were available in very limited numbers and there was a long waiting list. It was not unknown for the enterprising farmer to provide his own front wheels to make things a little easier and quieter. The original tractor wheel hub was used, but a discarded wheel rim from an old car was welded to it. The whole wheel centre was then filled with concrete to give it weight, and the conversion was complete. Uncle Fred Billing had a pair of these wheels fitted to his tractor for years.

For the first month or two after the declaration of War, nothing seemed to change very much. The radio was full of current affairs programmes and talk of what was going to happen on the home front in the not too distant future. Probably the first indications that all was not as it should be, were the black out restrictions for all houses and buildings.

The lighting restrictions for cars occupied most of our time at work. Headlights had to be partially blacked out for the first weeks, until the official blackout fittings became available. A few of these official masks eventually arrived from wholesalers, but not enough for the number of cars on the road. The only answer was to make some. They consisted of a blank plate to replace the glass, painted with a non-reflecting paint. Across the centre of this plate had to be cut a slot, not exceeding half an inch wide, and four inches long with a piece of frosted glass over the slot, on the inside. Over the outside of the slot a half round shield had to be fitted, with a plate at the front, so that no light would show above the car. Sidelight and rear light lenses had to be restricted to not more than one inch in diameter, by painting. It was almost a permanent job making and fitting the headlamp masks for many different size lamps. Later a white stripe two inches wide had to be painted all around each car used at night.

Lighting restrictions were not only applicable to cars, but motorcycles, and smaller versions had to be fitted to cycles. To ride without lights was still the subject of much shouting by the newly appointed special constables though.

The seriousness of the situation soon started to become evident when firms who had recently taken delivery of new vans and lorries found them confiscated for military use. There were no appeals or compensation, but it would all be sorted out after the war. Biscombes the ironmongers were the first to suffer, they had taken delivery of a new lorry on September 1st, but had it confiscated by 1st October. Large modern cars, suitable for staff cars were also taken for war use, which upset a number of ladies. How could they arrive at important functions in a small car?

Petrol ration coupons quickly followed. The ration was not enough to give people many miles of motoring. We had a hectic few days when people started to arrive with cans, bottles and tins to try to hoard a few gallons of any sort of petrol before rationing started. Once our stock of petrol ran out it was replaced by "Pool" petrol, a low-grade utility fuel. It did present some problems. Some cars could just not use it, and most engines had to have a minor adjustment.

There was some small compensation though. We could only have one underground tank filled with petrol, all the other tanks had to be sealed off for the duration. No more struggling with that Esso pump. Just the Dominion pump was in use, the lowest and most modern of the four pumps. Some essential users had to travel, regardless of what grade of petrol was available, and some with essential business uses for a car had extra ration coupons.

Quite a number of our regular customers thought it worthwhile to carry on running their cars, even if their mileage was restricted. People like Mr. Luke from Saltash, whose wife insisted on a weekly trip to Kit Hill for a walk. His immaculate Ford 8, reg number JY 3904 had to have a weekly oil level check, because it said so in the instruction book, even though he only drove about thirty miles a week.

Regular customers, and casual customers alike were very generous with tips, in those days, which helped to boost the weekly income. Doctor Jocelyn with his Austin Ten was a sure touch, especially if it was raining. As he pulled into the pump, off would come the coat while nipping out quickly to find out how many gallons he needed. After filling up he always asked the same question. "Where is your coat?" The reply was always the same. "Haven't got one Sir, can't afford it". He would struggle in his pocket and produce sixpence. A small fortune, a 3d piece was the usual tip, and it soon added up, if the stupid little coin didn't get lost.

In 1941 Dr Jocelyn changed his Austin for a slightly faster and sportier car, a Wolseley 12 HP Hornet Special, DPL 191. This car was fitted with a very Heath Robinson looking device to the petrol filler cap, which caused a lot of problems, just to get the cap off. Although the doctor was an old gent with snow-white hair, he did like to have a little burst of speed at times.

It wasn't long before Compulsory Military Service (call up) took away all the staff except Mr. Harrott and myself. With just the two of us left, meal breaks had to be taken in turns. There were a few customers who like to come and talk to the boss for an hour when they called for petrol. They always seem to call just as he was due to go for his dinner or his tea and it made my meals late. Gradually I learnt to recognise the sounds of their cars coming towards the garage, especially if they were coming from the Tavistock direction. Once I heard those cars coming I was able to tell him who was coming and get him out of the way. It took a long time for him to believe that I could recognise the sounds of all the cars.

Mr. Drew the vet, with his Morris Eight EAF 389, Harold Wilson the Insurance Inspector with his Ford 8 JY6219, Tom Martin from Brendon with his Austin 12 DRL873 and Bert Hearn from Cox Park with his Ford 8, BAT 357 were all easily recognised.

Mr. Barribal from Harrowbarrow and his two sons were always ready to stop and talk for an hour, and always seemed to pick the wrong time as far as my meal times were concerned. They had a Standard nine of about 1930 vintage PO9326 which was easily recognised, but when they changed to an Austin Ten Lichfield, RD 8208 it took a long time to get to know and I suffered.

Mrs. Mutton and her Austin Big Seven EAM 23 was a regular visitor, always during the late afternoon, just before teatime for Mr. Harrott. I did have problems learning the sound that little car.

We seemed to get a lot of visitors in the garage, mostly to just talk, or pass away an hour or two when they should be doing something else. One of these was Fred Townsend the newly appointed Special Constable. He would come and hide away inside our battery room door and have a crafty smoke. On one occasion, Mr. Harrott went to the front of the garage, and in a loud voice said "Your Constable, Inspector? Yes, he is in our battery room having a smoke and cup of tea". Fred put out his cigarette quickly and rushed out to find everybody having a laugh at his expense, and not an Inspector in sight. What we didn't know at the time was that in his rush to put out his cigarette, he burnt a hole in his Police issue raincoat, and had to pay for a new one. He didn't come again for a quiet smoke.

One gent who came every day and could not be moved was Mr. Dell from Florence Hill. He had a smallholding and sold the milk from his couple of cows to the householders around Moss Side. He walked around carrying a two gallon closed pail and a half pint measure hooked over the top rim, and dangling in the milk inside. On his other arm carried a few eggs in a large wicker basket with the eggs neatly packed in hay to stop them from knocking each other and breaking. At the end of his rounds he descended upon us to pass on any local gossip to the boss, and make his views about how the war should be fought to anybody who was unfortunate enough to get trapped. Not that he was an expert. During the First World War he worked in a farm. The pipe that he smoked, as he stood at the end of the bench and leaned on the drilling machine, was, to say the least, ripe. We made all kinds of excuses and made all kind of comments, but he always stood there and could not be insulted or made to take the hint, that he was not wanted there. Under the far end of the bench was an old magneto that we lit the welding torch with. Give the magneto a twist and it would produce a fat spark. I connected one lead to the bolt holding the drill to the bench, and then gave the magneto a twist. The poor old man gave a jump and wondered what had happened. We told him that he imagined it all, and would prove it by holding the drill. Of course there was no one turning the magneto. By the time Mr. Dell was convinced and was brave enough to lean on the drill again, there was someone to repeat the performance.

My working hours did not include Saturday afternoons off, but usually a Wednesday. Then I could get out on my ancient bike and see some of the places that I had never seen before. Working in the garage gave me access to a lot of spares that would normally by thrown away. Very lightweight front forks from small motorcycles ended up on my bike to make a softer if heavier ride. One day I would be able to afford a brand new bike.

With Wednesday afternoons free it was the intention to go and look up members of the family that we saw very little of. Father had a sister Beatrice who was married to George King. He was one of those little men that looked like monkeys painting the top of Saltash Bridge. He worked on that bridge for years. It was a job that never ended, as soon as the painters reached one end it was time to start all over again. The whole bridge was painted by hand, using four-inch brushes. At one time the Kings lived at Landrake, but later moved to Saltash. Their oldest son Young George I knew fairly well. He came to Tideford School for a year or two, after being expelled from Landrake. He always seemed to be up to mischief, in an innocent sort of way that somehow got out of hand. He had to leave Tideford School after the School bell got broken due to "hard contact with a stone thrown by the King Boy". The second son Jack, I don't seem to have had much contact with. The third son, Billy, was about my own age, and carried on the tradition of always being up to innocent mischief, and then things would go wrong.

Things were so much different then. Families lived within a few miles of each other but hardly made contact. Travel was difficult, and telephones were not the sort of thing that ordinary people had in their house in the late 1930s and none were available during the War. Despite all my good intentions, I saw very few of the family that were not around the Callington area.

Saturday afternoons were usually taken up by motorcyclists, who seemed to find that Saturdays were the only days they could find time for repairs. Mr. Friese from Pillaton and later from Linkinhorn, a huge man, worked as a forester for the Forestry Commission, always wanted either a tyre fitted or a new chain on his 500 cc Royal Enfield ALY 28 or so it appeared. A few weeks before war was declared Mr. Crago, a steam roller driver, took delivery of a new Ariel Square Four motor cycle combination, and came back every week just to be reassured that the little noise that he though he heard was perfectly normal. It was a beautiful machine though, all gleaming maroon paintwork and shining chrome, and it ran so smoothly and quiet. It was the only one of its kind in the district, and the envy of most motorcyclists who saw it.

The town saw changes almost daily, or so it seemed. Shopkeepers adapted themselves, with plenty of grumbling, about all those fiddly ration books and coupons. How on earth were they going to make a living if customers could not buy what they wanted?

All of a sudden the town became filled with children speaking a strange language, or so it seemed. Evacuees from the London and Norwich area were brought to our area for safety. What was the world coming to? They were all over the place, and had no respect for anybody or other people's property. If they were told off, they replied with a cheeky answer. But they did have ration books, and that meant more trade for the shops. It didn't take very long for the townsfolk to accept these children and make them feel at home. Their cheek was usually good-humoured fun to help to hide their fear and loneliness.

Gradually the smart cars that called at the garage for petrol on the way home from holidays just disappeared and we were left with the few locals who could still manage to keep their cars on the road. There were ways and means of course. For a time farmers had unrestricted use of petrol but not for private use. Old engines were in use for sawing wood or elevators, and old cars were used on the farm, the list of things farmers were able to invent to draw unrestricted petrol for was endless. Who can blame them if some petrol went into the car tank to help out the official ration?

Farmers, market gardeners and others who needed cars, vans or light lorries were in a difficult position as to what to buy. Would it be a fairly recent model or an old well tried model? If a recent model was bought, and something went wrong that required spare parts, there was the possibility that none would be available until after the War, whenever that was going to be. With an old model there was a very good chance of spares being available from scrap yards like George Orchards on Long Hill or maybe an old car lying around in someone's garage that could be bought, cheaply of course.

Uncle Jack from Kingsmill decided to buy a small lorry to go to market with the produce of his expanding market garden that was now large enough to employ his two sons Fred and Clifford. He elected to buy an old Chevrolet, converted from a touring car, and painted a vivid Blue with black chassis and wings. It was a quaint looking thing, and everybody thought that it was a bit of a joke. Much to everyone's amazement it went on for years with hardly any trouble and no major spares required.

Normal life went on, much the same as usual. On Tuesday nights Mrs. Strutt came over from Milbrook to open the cinema in Callington Town Hall. It was one weekly gathering that was usually well attended. Gene Autry was King of the cowboys then. We had our share of violent films of course. James Cagney and Pat O'Brien gave us the gangster films of the time. Where the baddies always lost. Too mild for Children's Hour today I suspect. Greta Garbo and Ann Gardner gave us our glamour films, while George Formby gave us laughs. Cinema visits were for entertainment and we were normally well entertained, mostly by comedy films. How things change.

The equipment was getting old in the Town Hall and occasionally, well, often, the film would stop due to some technical problem. When this happened there would be a lot of feet stamping and cries of "why are we waiting" from certain parts of the cinema. Mrs. Strutt, a very domineering type of lady, would go to the front, and threaten to throw everybody out if the noise carried on. No one was ever evicted, but the noise grew louder as she retreated to the little entrance hall, to resume her normal position of peering through the hole with gold lettering over the top, which identified it as the Box Office.

Most evenings I spent in the town, where all the teenagers met up to have a chat on Jane's corner, or to watch the girls go by. Gerald Pengelly, Bill Laundry, Albert Allen, Fernley Newcombe, Edward Giles, myself and quite a few others that had been at school together would meet up and maybe move on to the Working Men's Club, behind the Junior School, for a game of billiards or darts. The evening often finished off with a bag of chips and a bottle of Vimto at Gimblett's Fish and Chip shop in the market.

At work I began to notice how troublesome young lads could be, when you are busy. I can vividly remember a few boys being around one day when I was trying to do something at the front of the garage. Bill Pascoe from Dupath Road and Michael Williams were among them, giving out a bit of cheek. I threw a long tyre lever at them, but it was not a good enough throw. Mr. Harrott's Austin hire car was standing between myself and the boys. The tyre lever came down and made a long dent just above the rear side window. Of course the boys laughed and I didn't quite know what to do about it. The Boss was sure to see it. Perhaps I would leave things alone and hope for the best.

Several days went by and nothing was said. Shortly after, I was asked to give the car a quick clean, as it was being used for a wedding. I decided that now was as good a chance as I was ever going to get. After the clean I asked, in all innocence, what had happened to the bodywork above the rear window? After careful examination and thought, Mr. Harrott remembered that on a Taxi job one night recently, as he was going down a narrow lane, he heard a bump and had got out to investigate, but could find no damage, and then drove on. It never occurred to him to look so high up for damage. What luck.

By this time young men from the district were going off every day to join the Forces, and we teenagers looked at them with mixed feelings when they came to leave.

Every word of their adventures was listened to and dreamt about. All of a sudden, the town was full of soldiers. Almost overnight or so it seemed, a camp had been built beside the road at Kelly Bray and the land behind Glover and Uglows garage now had motor workshops among the trees, and a large compound where lorries, cars and motor cycles were stored. All those extra customers brought a smile to the faces of all the shopkeepers, even if the odd window did get broken with the night-time activities of some of the soldiers.

These troops did help the morale of the town though. There were frequent entertainments laid on in the Town Hall for their benefit, and there was always room for a few civilians, to see such names as Max Miller. An odd petrol coupon to Mrs. Strutt always helped to get in to see such shows. With the bombing of Plymouth, the town filled up with people looking for a safe place to sleep. The townspeople acted as would be expected, they squeezed together and made room for all comers.

Friends and relatives arrived and brought their friends with them. Empty fowl houses at Cox Park near Luckett were cleaned out and turned into temporary homes for the hundreds of people who came out of the City on that little single-track railway every night, in search of a safe night's sleep.

The walk home from town every night was a bit scary at times. There were no streetlights or friendly house lamps. The glow-worms kept their lights going though.

If I walked home over Florence Hill there was a grandstand view of all that was going on in Plymouth. Not only were the guns of Carkeel sounding as if they were in the next field, all the flashes were there too. Although we were about seven miles away from the guns, when they fired, the ground trembled.

Its no good denying it, we all got frightened at times. Was this war such an adventure after all? The blazing oil tanks at Torpoint were clearly visible, and it was as if they were just down the road. The whole City of Plymouth seemed to be on fire. From our vantage point high up on Florence Hill, all the searchlights that ringed the city could be seen, probing the air, looking for the rouge aircraft. Occasionally we would see an aircraft caught in the light, just like a shiny fly or insect trapped in a brilliant beam of light. Anti aircraft guns would open up, we could se the tracers flying skywards, but it was only on very rare occasions that we ever saw an aircraft brought down during an Air Raid.

Callington was only a few miles from Plymouth as the crow flies, or in this case as the Dornier bomber flies. The powers that be decided that an air raid siren should be installed, right away, for the protection of the townsfolk. A sire was duly obtained, but where was it to be fitted? On the Church Tower, or on the fire station roof? Maybe on a car roof so that it could tour the district and warn everybody? After over two hundred alerts the siren was fitted to the Fire Station, to call the firemen to a fire.......after the War.

A lot of things were changing. Almost every day there would be something different from the quiet sort of life we had become used to. But some things needed more than a mere war to make them change. Arthur Reed drove his horse and cart between Callington and his fields at Moss Side and Fullaford Road three or four times each day. If you spoke to Arthur, Jessie would stop. She knew that it was the signal to stop and talk. Arthur was never in a hurry, and knew everyone who walked or cycled along that stretch of road. He did like a good natter, to find out all the scandal and local gossip, to pass it on to the next person he met. Army convoys or lorries, tanks and guns, all had to travel at Jessie's pace of two miles an hour, or less, until there was a convenient place to overtake.

Aunt Ede and Uncle Vic from Elbridge were convinced that as they were only a very short distance from Plymouth and Saltash, they should come to our house at nights. Much easier, everyone agreed. Their house shook every time one of the huge guns at Carkeel was fired. The first night that they came to the house, three bombs were dropped just up the road, two in a field and one on the main road. Our house shook and I think every one of the tongue and grove timbers of thee lining opened up. After that they thought that they were safer in their own house.

Only one good thing came out of that bomb on the road. As it exploded our back door opened and in rushed Amy Williams who lived on Florence Hill, whose claim to fame was that she was considered to be one of the local beauties. When the first bomb dropped she was walking home along the road and ran to the nearest house. She must have taken all records with that sprint.

Then somebody had to be brave enough to walk her home.

CHAPTER 22 – A YEAR OLDER...OVERNIGHT

By the time that I was approaching my sixteenth birthday, there were not many jobs that I could tackle in the garage. Mr. Harrott was the only person to teach me, and he spent a lot of time at his post at the Royal Observer Corps, so I was left to make my own mistakes, and learn by them. Garage work was far different then than it is today. Car engines needed decarbonising and the valves reground about every six thousand miles, a thing no longer heard of. Re-boring and new pistons were fitted at about forty thousand miles at the most. With the use of Pool Petrol, these mileages were reduced considerably, so I was kept busy. All these repairs depended on a supply of spare parts, which were fast becoming a thing of the past, so spares had to be taken from laid up vehicles, making extra work. Cars of the day all seemed to suffer from rear axle troubles. To fit new Crown wheels and Pinions were a normal occurrence, a task never even thought about today.

I mentioned earlier the different oils that we kept and how I had to learn which engines used different oils. With wartime shortages, there had to be some compromise with oils. Castrol XL and XXL were the "in" oils, which we normally kept in five gallon drums laid on their side with a tap fitted to the filler hole. XL, XXL and Castrolite were kept in a cabinet on the forecourt with the half pint, pint and quart measures on a tray at the bottom. Esso oil was stored in a three-tier cabinet, with the three grades of oil, Light, Medium and Heavy in pint bottles with different coloured caps. The other oil we stocked was Pratts in two grades, light and heavy. These were very cheap oils and normally used in well-worn engines, so that it didn't get used so fast. This was stored and sold from a square cabinet with two pumps at the top, covered at night by a sliding cover. In frosty or very cold weather the oil in these pumps became so thick and heavy that it couldn't be pumped out. Any engine that used this oil had to be kept indoors overnight during very cold weather. The oil would become so thick that the engine could not be turned over to start it. When it was used by farmers who were now starting the use Fordson tractors, they had to light small fires under the engines when they were left out overnight.

We did keep another oil, "Superoil", which was a reclaimed oil, from a small refining workshop in Bristol, owned by a man called Wild, who wore all the firm's hats. As well as being owner and managing director, he was the chief chemist, production manager and salesman. He visited our little garage in his capacity as Salesman. He drove a huge Humber car, and always had a young dolly bird with him. Each time he came there was a different girl and Mr. Harrott was convinced that all the girls in Bristol had blonde hair, long legs and had been in this car at some time. He was always referred to as being Wild by name and by nature. He always drove very fast, with a huge capacity for whatever spirit he could get hold of. He must have been almost blind as well. When taking an order, the pen and order book would be held almost at the tip of his nose, so that he could see what he had written. This oil was produced in the same grades as Castrol but never ordered for sale to the public. Unlike other oils, there were no shortages. When Castrol became scarce we could only buy it in forty-gallon drums, not very convenient when it had to be transferred to five-gallon drums for us to sell it. However "Superoil" being in the same grades as Castrol and supplied in ten-gallon drums, was much easier to handle. Somehow, they got mixed up and nobody ever noticed the difference.

Esso was no longer supplied in their tall distinctive, one and two pint bottles. It now came in forty-gallon drums. It was so much easier to fill the bottles from a ten-gallon drum with a fitted tap, even if the drum was marked "Superoil".

Pratts never changed, it still came in tall coned returnable drums with steel bands around the outside, so there was no need for any changes.

I was able to realise one of my ambitions just before my sixteenth birthday. A new bike. Trewartha Gregory and Dodge had three Guarantor bikes in stock, and I could afford one. No more going around with a nose pressed hard against the shop windows, looking for something that took your fancy that could be afforded. Tall, sit up and beg, with rod brakes, and no gears, and all for only £4 2/6. But it was mine. For £2 I bought an extra good dynamo lighting set, although there were lighting restrictions, and it was not possible to use the good light that was produced.

This gave me the opportunity to make and sell my very first invention. The blank disc that we had to fit either inside, outside or in place of the normal lens was only allowed a small diameter hole for light, not enough to see anything with. My disc was extended a little at the top to allow it to be made into a small hinge. This was attached to a band around the rim of the lamp. It was held in the "down" position by a small spring for regulation use. When you were out of the way of Air Raid

Wardens and Police, the front disc could be turned "up" and held in place by the same spring. You could enjoy a good light, and see all those hidden potholes in the road. There was a ready sale at 2/6d each (2 ½ p).

When Mr. Harrott went off to his Observer Corps he thought of very little else, and completely forgot about the customer's cars that were parked outside on a bit of hard standing. The Police decided that lights were required if cars were parked there after dark. It was my job to get them inside. I had never been taught to drive, and neither did I have a licence to drive along the short bit of road to the garage property. With very few paint scratches that were noticed, I learnt to drive this way, just moving cars in and out of the garage. There was only one that I could not move without instructions. Mr. Ed Snell from St Dominic brought his old Model "TT" Ford Lorry in for servicing and that was something different to all other cars and vans. It was fitted with "Epicyclic" gearbox as standard. Once the engine was started, if the handbrake was released fully you were in top gear. Low gear was achieved by holding a foot pedal down to the floorboards. Not easy when the lorry had a load and a steep hill to negotiate. The whole weight of the load was transferred to the driver's leg and somehow you had to hold it in gear. A short piece of wood was usually kept handy to fix between the foot pedal and the wooden seat front. You will notice that I did say "once the engine was started". This was not easy on this model. The usual practice was to lift the rear wheels off the ground with the quick lift jacks supplied with the vehicle. The handbrake would be released, the choke pulled out and the hand throttle on the steering wheel hub set in the correct position. With blocks in front of the front wheels it only needed cranking with the starting handle and a lot of luck. The whole transmission and engine would turn over as one unit, and if it started the whole lorry would shake and rattle, sometimes shaking itself off the jacks, and relying on the front wheel blocks to stop it from going forward. It did this to me once, while it was in front of the garage. Unfortunately the blocks didn't hold, and the whole lot went forward, through the asbestos end wall, and ended up with the front wheels in mid air where the floor had been raised four feet to make it level above the sloping ground.

This old lorry was a curiosity even in those days, and I recall Dr Jocelyn's wife saying, "Does that thing really work?" But it was Mr. Snell's pride and joy. Every time it was brought in for repair it came complete with spare parts list, with a list of the optional extras available when it was new. One such extra was head and tail lamps, either acetylene or oil powered. Side-lamps were already fitted.

The day came when I had to send off my Five Shillings and an application form to get my motorcycle Driving Licence, to start on my sixteenth birthday. I had to wait another year before I could apply for a Licence to drive a car. How stupid of me to put my date of birth down as 1924 instead of 1925. Now I could drive cars and test them for myself. No Driving Test in those days, just good luck and good brakes.

The family connections all changed around as the war went on. Aunt Win, mother's young sister, got married to Harry Higman, who came home from serving in India with the Army. They went to live at 10 Church Street, Callington. Uncle Art had got married again and worked for Watkins and Reseveare at Ivybridge. They were Agricultural Engineers and the largest supplier of tractors and implements around.

At the beginning of the war the directors did most of the work, except repairs. Mr. Roseveare was the salesman and Ken Watkins was the lorry driver. Mr. Roseveare was a big Chapel man and prominent Liberal. Before long they had a further branch at Liskeard where Eric Billing worked in the workshops, after finding that there were better ways of earning a living than sat on a tractor ploughing someone's field. Arthur Billing was the Ivybridge lorry driver. Cecil was not satisfied to be tied in to a hairdressing business and always wanted to do something more creative. He joined Watkins and Roseveare, as a welder. Brother Ray went to the Liskeard branch to learn Agricultural Engineering, and travelled to and fro on a little Coventry Eagle 146cc motorbike JY 6486 made with a pressed steel frame.

One thing that never changed was the uncanny way that all the family or so it seemed, got to know that there were always hot pasties for tee on Saturdays at Sunnyside. Every Saturday the visitors would arrive, but mother never complained. Instead of making individual pasties she would make maybe four large round meat and potato pasties. When they were cut the gravy would run out of them and that lovely smell would drift around the house. Any that was left over would be reserved for Sunday night. Cold pasty with brown sauce had its fans too. As Grand Father Billing had retired and lived at Bush cottages, just under Kit Hill Castle he used to walk down for a chat on Saturdays. He was a strong Labour supporter. Uncle Vic was a strong Liberal. Uncle Fred would support any side that needed some support in their argument. There were some heated discussions at times and Vic would push his hat back, and scratch his head in frustration, whilst Uncle Fred would do a grin and start another controversial discussion. Granfer would puff harder on his pipe and slap the arm of the chair, to make a point...... Things got quite heated and noisy at times.

Ron, Arthur Billing's son was living with us as one of the family and went to the Grammar School at Callington. There were times that mother almost threw her arms in the air with despair. She wasn't at all pleased when she found Ron doing his metalwork homework on her sideboard. It wouldn't have been so bad if it had been paper work, but practical work with a hammer and a piece of copper to make a comb tray didn't meet with approval.

Life in the garage was getting a bit hectic with few spares and no help. First job in the mornings was to collect the keys from Mr. Harrot's house and unlock. With no mains electricity, the only way of keeping a decent light in the workshop or use the petrol pump was to keep the storage batteries fully charged. In a corner was an old Trojan flat twin engine that many years previously had been the power under a Brooke Bond Tea van. I say "under" because that is where the engine was fitted, under the seat of the van. The radiator had been replaced by a forty-gallon oil drum with water inlets at top and bottom. On the concrete base that held the engine in place was mounted a dynamo to charge the storage batteries. Fixed to the wall were two fuel tanks, one small one that held about half a gallon, and the other a tank removed from under the bonnet of an old Morris Cowley that held eight gallons. The method of starting was to grab the flywheel (that had a belt attached to turn the dynamo) and turn the engine over by pulling the flywheel around. Only one carburettor full of petrol was normally needed to get the engine going, before turning over to the larger of the tanks that was filled with paraffin.

Once started it would run all day with that distinctive noise beside you all the time. By about 4.30 pm it would be so very hot that the fuel could be turned off, and the battery removed from the ignition, and it would continue to run for over an hour due to the pre-ignition from the hot spots inside the cylinder head.

110 volts was sufficient for lighting but there was no garage equipment that would run on such low voltage. Any drilling required had to be done by hand using an assortment of ancient drills. Grinding, including the sharpening of drills was carried out by a foot-operated grindstone, fitted to the end of the bench. All work under cars was carried out lying on your back underneath the car. No ramps in those days, just a hydraulic jack and two axle stands. A pit was not practical. It would be full of water most of the time. As the garage floor, although smooth, was built on a slope, when it rained the water from the road flowed through the large front doors, and through the workshop. During the winter the floor was permanently wet.

Life seemed to be getting full of things that needed doing from now on. At the ripe old age of sixteen, I was allowed to join the L.D.W. later renamed the Home Guard. One night a week we had to go to the Territorial Army Drill Hall in the Market place to learn all about being part time soldiers, and get to know the weapons that one day we might see and use. We learnt Arms Drills with two or three official imitation rifles, except for people like father who had a shotgun of his own to drill with. We did eventually gat a rifle each........and a uniform. Jim Flashman, who lived next door to us at Blunts when I was very young, turned up as the Sergeant in charge, and father was my Lance Corporal.

There was the odd occasion when we had to spend a night out on exercise, or if there was a scare of invasion. On one occasion I found myself on some exercise on Kit Hill all night. When the van had delivered father and myself to the little makeshift observation hut with a field telephone, we got ready to spend the night as comfortably as possible. After a cup of tea and a sandwich, father settled down and lit up his pipe. By this time of life I had learnt to smoke the same as everybody else. When I went to light up my Woodbine, I had no matches. Still it was alright, father had some. When I asked him for a match he said, "Who taught you to smoke son?" Quickly I replied, "I did". "The same one must teach you to buy matches too," was his reply. That was the end of that conversation, and my smoking that night, but I was never without matches again.

There were light moments, even when things in the war looked bad. When cars were left they had to be immobilised. Removing the key was not enough if you were going to be more than a few yards away. There were still a lot of cars that didn't have keys, only switches. On modern cars people removed rotor arms from distributors. Various means of immobilising cars were devised. It was not unusual to see someone walking around with an easily removed gear lever in their hand. One of the Special Constables who had been a bit of an odd job man before the war was trying to be very good at the job, with his little bit of newfound authority. Fred Townsend never did like work. He knew where I worked and would keep asking if a particular car was immobilised or not. If it was to the advantage of our group of lads to know where he was for an hour or two I would have a look and tell him that it wasn't. He would then wait beside the car, convinced that he had a catch, until the owner returned, with half of his car in his pocket.

Most of the fruit wholesalers who came up form Cornwall for the strawberries had found that either they could not get the petrol to come, or that their main source of income, holiday makers, were no longer around. One or two still came, among them a Mr. and Mrs. Wakeham from Bodmin. On one occasion their old Vauxhall car broke down and was beyond repair. They eventually bought Mr. Harrott's big Wellesley 21/60 OD 8993, ideal for their use, as they ran a farm as a sort of sideline to get petrol. Mr. Harrott then bought a 1935 Austin 18/6 limousine, C M

C4, that eventually was going to be the car used to carry me to my wedding to the girl I had not yet met.

Some fruit and vegetable wholesalers were more fortunately located. Bill Hooper and his new wife May lived in a bungalow on Long Hill when they got married. He ran a Ford Lorry to take goods to market, as well as collecting milk for the Creamery at Saltash. For local runs he had a 1938 Austin 7 van that, to say the least, was not in the best of condition. I was offered the chance to do a bit of driving a "couple of nights a week", going around to fruit growers and buying fruit, mostly strawberries.

Within a week or two I found that this was for five nights a week, and not only to buy the fruit but to take it to Launceston and Holsworthy to sell it, all after leaving work at the garage at five o'clock. I must admit though that the fruit had only to be taken to two shops to dispose of a full load. It was hard work, travelling all around St Dominic, Harrowbarrow and Metherell, before setting off for Devon. When the strawberry season had finished, apples took their place, but I only had to travel to Launceston with them. To earn about three pounds a week was good, even if I didn't get home until the early hours of the morning.

Mother always waited up to make sure that I got in safely and there was always a hot drink waiting. The air was so still and clear in that area, with virtually no traffic noise around she could hear the distinctive tinkling of the centre caps of the wheels as I was coming across the level ground some three miles away.

The shortage of spare parts certainly affected the condition of the little green Austin van. At the best of times brakes on any Austin 7 overloaded, as we often were, left the chances of stopping almost nil. One place where fruit had to be delivered to was in the middle of a very steep hill in Launceston, where Mr. Miller, the shopkeeper lived. As it was always late at night before I arrived there, they were willing to suffer the inconvenience of fruit delivered to their home rather than have none to sell. The little van also suffered from a minor gearbox problem. It would slip out of gear under the load. The combination of defects made it impossible to stop outside their house. We had an arrangement. At the top of the hill I would stop, put the van in low gear and hold it in position with a piece of wood, made for the purpose. The hand brake would be full on, and the brake pedal kept as hard down as possible. As I passed their house, the horn would be blown continuously and I would go past to the bottom of the hill. Not very fast, probably, only about two or three miles an hour, but I just could not stop completely. From the bottom of the hill I would reverse back to the house, and if all went well, someone would be waiting with a block of wood. All I had to do then was to ease gently forward on to the block.

At this time of the war, sweets and chocolates were severely rationed, so "an arrangement" was made that if the shop in Holsworthy wanted fruit, we wanted chocolate. Once a week the passenger seat of the little van was lifted up and a stock of goodies would be packed in the little box underneath for consumption at Callington.

Under the driver seat there would be packed a two-gallon can of paraffin and a pint tin of petrol. To start the van when I picked it up after work would entail removing the float chamber of the carburettor and filling it with petrol. This would normally be sufficient to start the engine. From then on it would run on paraffin, hopefully. All strictly illegal of course. If the engine was allowed to stop and go in the least bit cool the whole procedure had to be gone through again, hence the pint of petrol.

Even going as far as Holsworthy with fruit was illegal. There was a limit of fifteen miles in which soft fruit could be sold, and Holsworthy was about twenty-eight miles from Callington. Even after a journey of that length, the smell of paraffin coming out of the exhaust could not be mistaken for anything else.

There were other defects such as light that failed to work, and the absence of door catches that always helped to put a little spice into life. Covering the rear number plate with mid, so that the police at Launceston could not read it was normal. I recall on one occasion when the rear doors burst open going over a hump backed bridge, and the full load of two hundred baskets of strawberries fell on to the road. I cannot recall who was with me on this occasion, I think it was Frank Clarke from Clawton, but we picked them all up as best we could and delivered them in the dark as usual. We were only three baskets short.

The next time I went with a delivery the shopkeeper remarked that the last lot appeared a bit gritty. I wonder why?

Between Home Guard, driving the van and work there was not much spare time, but somehow the young men of the town would get together and have a chat, and watch the girls go by as usual. Now the girls had soldiers to interest them so most of the local lads were feeling a little left out of things.

The talk would eventually turn to the main subject. Would we be called up and what would we do if that day came? Would it be Army, Navy or Air Force, if we were given the choice? Some of us could, if we wished, claim exemption from going off to war. It was a problem that occupied our minds almost continuously, and a decision would shortly have to be made. I was fortunate in some respects, though. I had plenty of work that I enjoyed to occupy my mind.

I wasn't all that keen on all the running around, playing silly games that the Home Guard seemed to be keen on. Eventually for no reason that I know of, except that I held a Motor Cycle driving licence, I was informed that I was to be the Official Despatch Rider for the Company. Now that was a morale booster. The following Sunday morning I was taken to Kelly Bray by Jim Flashman to collect he motorbike. After filling up with petrol and signing a sheaf of forms to say that I had received the machine I was allowed to take it away.

The engine started easily and I sat astride the bike and gently freewheeled down the slope from the Army storage Depot, through Glover And Uglows yard, to the main road. From there I freewheeled across the road to Redmore Road, where there was no one around. No way was I going to admit to the Army, the Home Guard or anyone else that the most powerful motorcycle I had ridden was a little 145cc two-stroke, and never one with a foot change. Here I was with a brand new Ariel 350 cc ohv with foot change and I had to ride the thing expertly. After a few hair raising take off attempts, and a few wobbly rides up and down the road I felt a bit more confident, and eventually got it back to the drill hall, a little later than everyone had expected. Home Guard exercises were a little more interesting after that.

The shortage of new vans was beginning to make itself felt. There were plenty of good hardly used cars available, mostly laid up and on blocks, which owners were willing to sell.

Many were for sale at silly prices, especially if the owner had to pay garage fees to park their pride and joy, or if the owner faced the prospects of leaving it out in the open for who knows how many years. I can clearly remember Derek Warwick trying to sell his beautiful old Citroen salon, on the day before he had to join the Army, for the princely sum of two pounds. No one could foresee the value of these cars after the war and they would have been worth storing. Getting rid of it was top priority for everybody. There seemed to be no point in keeping a car lying around for maybe years.

CHAPTER 23 – TIME TO GO...

There were a number of slightly older cars off the road that would make good vans if a new body were available. The essential requirement was that it had to have a real chassis, not one of the modern 'strengthened bodywork' jobs as Mr. Harrott called them. Austin 12s or 16s were excellent for the job. As if we didn't have enough work to do we had to start stripping the old bodywork off these old cars and giving the chassis a coat of paint. The chassis were then sent to Henwoods of St Anne's Chapel, for them to build a new wooden body. The bottom half was made of solid timber, whilst the top half had a lightweight frame only. Over this framework was stretched a canvas cover, that was painted to match the rest of the bodywork. That type of van became very popular and helped many small businesses to carry on during the war.

With the demands for more food to be produced the Market Gardens of the Tamar Valley were producing other foods than strawberries and flowers. As the fields were too steep to plough by horse or by light tractor and extra land had to be cultivated more we had to be use what implements were available. Old, powerful cars were in great demand and we had a regular job converting them.

Stripped bare of all the bodywork, an extra gearbox was fitted behind the normal gearbox to give a very low gear to the rear wheels. The car was then positioned at the top of the field and the rear jacked up. A drum, loaded with a wire rope was fitted to one wheel. With a suitable pulley fitted to a movable anchor point at the top of the field the wire rope would be attached to a light plough at the bottom and winched to the top, then returned to the bottom for the next furrow. Work such as this kept us busy to compensate for the private car work that had become almost extinct.

The weekend of March 20/21st 1942 was the weekend of a large scale Home Guard exercise, where the Army was going to become involved. The Home Guard Commander, Mr. Blight, lived in a large house, Chequets Hall, in Church Street. This was to be the centre of operations. I cannot recall what happened on the Saturday night, but I do recall that Sunday morning found me, as Despatch Rider, standing outside the Commander's Office waiting for messages to deliver. On the Army bike of course.

Down the passage came a lovely little Parlour Maid, all dressed up with her little white cap, and white starched apron. She carried a tray, which I knew meant tea at last, and I needed it. We can always dream though. She smiled and walked straight past to Mr. Blights office. Never mind she would come back with mine later. But no, no tea for the boys. The same happened three or four times that day, and I was glad when the exercise was called off in the late afternoon. I don't think I even got a ride on the motorbike that day.

My prize was yet to come though. That first smile had led to more smiles and a few words. That evening in the street, Betty Tucker went to Underhills the Chemist for some Aspro. When she came out, I happened to be outside. It ended up with a walk around the "Island" and arrangements for a further meeting.

When I was delivering fruit and vegetables for Ralph Deacon I had delivered to her mother a few times, so I felt that I had a little bit of advantage. Her father was a baker for the N.A.A.F.I and worked in Devonport, and only came home at weekends.

Petticoat government soon followed. Give up some of the night driving or else........ Willingly I modified my driving hours to only two nights a week. On those two nights Betty came with me to go around St Dominic before I set off for Launceston. It wasn't very romantic, trips out in that smelly old van, but she didn't mind that too much. The method of securing the doors with a piece of rope all round the van didn't seem quite right to her, but as long as it was only me that had to climb in and out of the drivers window, she didn't object.

I met with approval with her family, and she fitted in with my family and met with full approval. So it seemed that we were on the way for great things in the future. Her mother was not quite so sure when one evening we went out in Bill Hooper's Ford lorry to collect potatoes and became stranded in a field until very late, because the load was not ready. I don't think we ever told her mother about how the van ran backwards down a hill near Cothele Quay, while Bet was in the passenger seat, and the back of the van was filled with apples. At the time I was outside paying the grower for the apples. Well, I did say the brakes were not too good.

At home, there was a sort of routine around the fields. Spring would bring out the flowers to send off to market, although the problems involved with sending very many to Covent Garden by bus and train hardly made it worthwhile. Fruit and vegetables were always required by the local shops and the Plymouth Markets, and were much easier to reach.

By now we had poultry houses all over the "top field" and what seemed like thousands of fowls running around. On the surface, keeping a few fowls seemed to be an easy way of earning a living, but it was hard work. Houses had to be cleaned out almost daily. Fowls had to be fed at least twice a day if eggs were to be produced. Three or four times a day, eggs had to be collected from the nest boxes built along the sides and rear of the fowl's houses, to say nothing of the nests that some fowls insisted on making for themselves in some remote tuft of grass or under some piece of machinery. There were hazards when eggs were collected. Most fowls would be quite happy and contented when you lifted the outside flap to put your hand in to collect the eggs from the hay lined nest box, where the majority of hens laid their eggs. If you were obliged to put your hand under any hen who was the temporary occupant of a nest box, some hens were quite happy about such an intrusion. Others took a different view, and would give a very hard and definite peck at the back of the hand that dared to intrude at such a very private moment.

Father's cats were everywhere, and the poultry took no notice of them. When the weather turned a bit chilly it was not unusual to find a cat curled up in one of the nest boxes, enjoying a warm sleep in the hay that was meant for the hens to lay their eggs in.

Most memories of Sunnyside are of fine, warm sunny days, with the fields full of poultry. There are not many countryside sounds that can compare with the sound of a few hundred contented hens, singing and cackling in a sunlit field on a summer's day.

There were other sides of poultry keeping too. At one stage we almost had to obtain permission to enter our fields from the big red rooster that considered himself king. He had the courage of a gladiator, and was willing to do battle with anybody. He would attack from any vantage point, the roof of a hen house or the top of a gatepost where his favourite spots. When he attacked there were wings, beaks and spurs everywhere, and he could inflict real damage. To say nothing of the loss of dignity when you had to admit to being floored by a red rooster.

The house was dominated to a certain extent by eggs. All those eggs that were collected had to be washed, dried, examined for defects, graded into size and packed. Cracked eggs were made into sponges that the cats would steal at every opportunity, or else made into delicious bacon and egg tarts. Others were given to father's cats to "make their coats shine". Small or odd shaped eggs went into the frying pan for breakfast.

Mother would spend hours cleaning those eggs, and became a master at getting any unwary visitor to join in, as she rubbed stubborn mark off with a spot of Vim. Bet was among them. Not many people got away.

Boxes containing fifteen dozen eggs, all in separate cardboard sections, lined the wall of the scullery to wait collection on Monday mornings by the van from the Egg Packing Station at Moss Side or Culleys of Kelly Bray.

Bet and I seemed to be spending most of our time together, just walking and talking. The future was a bit uncertain. We didn't talk about it much, but just assumed that if there was going to be a future we would spend it together. Kit Hill was a favourite spot, for long talks and being alone, but it was a long walk home if you left it a bit late. She did like dancing, but it was one thing that I could never do, owing to a deformity from birth. I was blessed with two left feet. I must admit that I used to like going to the Blue Cap dances on a Saturday night, and listen to the music. Now a new type of music was coming out of the Ballroom, and a new type of dancing. The foxtrot had given way to dances where girls were being thrown all over the place, and dance bands had a completely new sound. The Americans were everywhere and their music was something that seemed to bring new life to tired old towns like Callington.

I was going to be eighteen and due for a call up at any time after June 12th. A lot of friends had gone off to the forces, some had got deferments, and others like Bill Laundry had gone and would never return. Various members of the family had already gone off to do their bit in the war. Earnest Heath had been recalled to the Navy and father's brother Harry had also been recalled as an Instructor. Bernard Olding had joined the Air Force and Clifford Billing who had every reason for not joining up was away in the Army. He had been badly burned as a child and only had some stumps where his fingers should have been. He served all through the war to be killed by a train on a level crossing in Yorkshire after demob.

His brother Fred stayed at home to work on the land. Bernard Billing stayed at home for the same reason. Ritchie Oliver was deferred as he worked on the railways. Father's older brother Bert was in the dessert with Montgomery during the war. He came home to be killed whilst making the large car park at Looe.

Bet's brother Tom was in Canada with the R.A.F.

Bet was so good for me in those days. She even gave up her dancing so that we could spend more time together. She gave up her job in Mr. Blight's big house and went to work in the Office of Trewartha Gregory and Doidge in Church Street. That was more good news. I could always find an excuse to go to that shop during the dinner hour.

At last it happened. The dreaded buff envelope that we knew would come one day. Now it was decision time. There was pressure to do both things.

Go into the Forces and risk everything being the same when I came home, or take Mr. Harrott's offer up of getting a deferment, on the grounds that we did agricultural work repairing tractors and War Agricultural Lorries from the Prisoner of War Camp that had been set up at Moss Side.

My mind was made up for me by the girl who meant more to me than anything else. She said that she would still be there when I came home.

On September 12th 1943, just two weeks after my apprenticeship had officially been completed, we climbed that hill from Sunnyside to Kelly Bray together, for me to catch the Kelly Bray Express to the great unknown world, away from home and all that was so good, to face an uncertain future.

H. M King George wanted me to train as an Air Mechanic in the Fleet Air Arm, and earn lots of money. Well to be exact it was 21/- a week (£1.05p). On the train I met up with two Cornishmen from the Lizard, and Tommy Williams from Plymouth. When we got to H.M.S Gosling the training school, near Warrington, the first thing we saw, beside the Main Entrance was a green yard.

We all looked at each other and made a decision. It was a very definite and serious decision, and we were willing to abide by the outcome. We would ask the first person we saw to toss a coin, to decide if we would go in, or turn around and take a chance on the future. Heads we lost, and we would go in and hope for the best, tails we won and would go home…. Or somewhere. The first person we saw was someone else going to join up. He tossed the coin.

WE LOST, but that's another story.

ABOUT THE AUTHOR

W J H Olding (known as Jack to his friends and family) died in 2005, but left a small collection of his work in hand printed books and booklets. More of his stories are being prepared for publication in the near future.

Printed in Great Britain
by Amazon.co.uk, Ltd.,
Marston Gate.